D1223565

POLITICAL CHANGE IN
EASTERN EUROPE SINCE 1989

POLITICAL CHANGE IN EASTERN EUROPE SINCE 1989

Prospects for Liberal Democracy and a Market Economy

Robert Zuzowski

Westport, Connecticut
London

Library of Congress Cataloging-in-Publication Data

Zuzowski, Robert.
    Political change in Eastern Europe since 1989 :   prospects for
liberal democracy and a market economy / Robert Zuzowski.
       p.   cm.
    Includes bibliographical references (p.   ) and index.
    ISBN 0–275–96145–1 (alk. paper)
    1. Europe, Eastern—Politics and government—1989- 2. Former
Soviet republics—Politics and government. 3. Europe, Eastern—
Economic policy—1989- 4. Former Soviet republics—Economic
policy. I. Title.
JN96.A58Z89   1998
320.947′09′049—dc21   97–32998

British Library Cataloguing in Publication Data is available.

Library of Congress Catalog Card Number: 97–32998
ISBN: 0–275–96145–1

First published in 1998

Praeger Publishers, 88 Post Road West, Westport, CT 06881
An imprint of Greenwood Publishing Group, Inc.

Printed in the United States of America

The paper used in this book complies with the
Permanent Paper Standard issued by the National
Information Standards Organization (Z39.48–1984).

10 9 8 7 6 5 4 3 2 1

The financial assistance of the Centre for Science Development
(HSRC, South Africa) toward this research is hereby acknowledged.
Opinions expressed and conclusions arrived at are those of the author and
are not necessarily to be attributed to the Centre for Science Development.

For my late parents

Little else is requisite to carry a state to the highest degree of opulence from the lowest barbarism, but peace, easy taxes, and a tolerable administration of justice; all the rest being brought about by the natural course of things.

—Adam Smith, *Wealth of Nations*

Contents

1. Introduction   1

2. Eastern Europe After the Collapse of Communism   13

3. Russia: Carpetbaggers' Country   47

4. Poland: Spin-Doctors' State   71

5. Czech Republic: Czechs Are Different   97

6. The West's Approach to Postcommunist Eastern Europe   119

7. Conclusion: Eastern European Prospects for Liberal
    Democracy and a Market Economy   141

    Selected Bibliography   149

    Index   161

1   Introduction

The process of the collapse of communism began in Poland in mid-1989. Soon it spread to other East European countries and, by the end of 1991, to the Soviet Union itself, a country where communism had its birth. Shortly afterward three multinational states in the area, namely, Yugoslavia, Czechoslovakia, and the Soviet Union, ceased to exist. The Soviet empire, the last surviving colonial power, crumbled almost overnight and without much bloodshed. In its place, many new independent nation-states emerged, some for the first time.

The fall of communism, the demise of the Soviet empire, and the breakdown of the Soviet Union itself constitute some of the most important events in twentieth-century political history and beyond. Although communism is dead in this part of the world, the region's political and economic future is not a foregone conclusion, notwithstanding many claims to the contrary. This book is about political change in Eastern Europe *after* the collapse of communism; it comprises the period from the late 1980s to the late 1990s. The detailed discussion that follows a general examination of the region is narrowed down to three countries: Russia, Poland, and the Czech Republic. The analysis is limited to a few countries only because to examine the entire region country by country—over two dozen states—would make for tedious reading and an overlapping and rather superficial text.

Why these particular states were chosen for discussion relates to their significance. The choice of Russia is obvious: It remains the largest state in the world, and though militarily and economically weakened recently, it is nonetheless a nuclear power to be reckoned with. In reality, Russia never experienced democracy before the demise of communism, which makes a discussion of its prospects for a stable, liberal democracy interesting and difficult at the same time. The political development in Russia will, most likely, continue to have international or even global ramifications, and this is an additional reason for taking it into consideration.

Poland is the country where the fall of communism began. It is a medium European state in terms of its size and population, positioned between Germany and the former Soviet republics. World War II started here. It has very little experience of democracy and a market economy, and in these respects it is similar to most other East European states and the former Soviet republics. In many ways Poland is a typical East European country.

The Czech Republic is different if not unique: Between World Wars I and II, Czechoslovakia (of which the Czech lands were a part) was the *only* democratic, industrialized country in Eastern Europe. Does its past make the Czech Republic's prospects for a liberal democracy and market economy significantly better than those of other Eastern European states? Does history matter in relation to present and future developments? If yes, how far back in time should one go when discussing today's and tomorrow's political development? These are the questions that make the choice of this country nearly obligatory, the more so because most political and economic analysts in the West devote so little attention to it, focusing their interest for some obscure reasons on Hungary, which is rather a typical East European state.

Many East European states now try to achieve two goals simultaneously—those of a liberal democracy and a market economy. With regard to a transformation from a command to a market economy, note that in Eastern Europe World War II and the imposition of communism in its aftermath did not destroy modern market economies; they never existed there before. Once again Czechoslovakia is an exception that proves the rule. Of course, the process toward the introduction of a communist economy began in Russia soon after the Bolshevik seizure of power in 1917—much earlier than in the rest of Eastern Europe.

Once communism collapsed in Eastern Europe, its people returned, at least initially, to what they knew already, namely, to the modus operandi in politics and economics from the precommunist era. This widely observed phenomenon proves once again that old habits die hard, and that it is rather easier to teach those who know nothing about a certain skill that we intend to teach them, than to teach them to use in a new way a skill they already possess.

Thus it follows that for the East Europeans to achieve their new goals will now be difficult because of their habits: old and bad as well. Their business habits are more reminiscent of a street beggar than of a "poor man." Most people would probably agree with the view that whether one gives a street beggar a few bucks or several thousand dollars he might stop begging, for a while, until he spends all his money on consumer goods, without even bothering to become financially independent when the opportunity arose. Why? Because to beg is more a way of life than anything else. The opposite relates to a poor man who became poor not from choice but because of unhappy circumstances. Western Europe was a "poor man" in the wake of World War II, captive to circumstances, whereas Eastern Europe is a "street beggar" as a matter of choice, whether conscious of it or not.

Of course, East Europeans will always deny this, and most of them would really be surprised to hear such an unorthodox view. But a real street beggar will also, without much doubt, deny it. For to deny this claim is in his best interests, and he knows it well. Once he admits to choice, he will almost certainly receive no more alms.

To move rapidly from poverty to wealth for an entire nation amounts to a near miracle; it comes close to creating something out of nothing. Little wonder that the field of social science called economics was once described as a "dismal science." Why? The reason becomes clearer today when economics tries to deal with the problems Eastern Europe faces at present. Not only do Westerners think they can solve Eastern European problems, the East Europeans think likewise.

The Eastern Europeans' rather tacitly assumed belief concerning political and economic transformation from communism to liberal democracies and market economies is predicated on a fundamental, yet largely incorrect, premise that, stated bluntly, is as follows: "We can do it." That is to say, by ourselves we are able to change our communist system successfully in a relatively short time. This assumption, in most East European cases, is wrong. No precedent exists for it; indeed, all our historical knowledge points the other way: Market economies, functioning well with sustained high growth and development, are improbable and rare. To build a rapidly prospering market economy based on a stable liberal democracy in most former communist countries has little chance of success in the near future.

Of course, the chances of success vary from country to country. Chances are greater, for instance, in a country such as the Czech Republic, which between world wars was a highly industrialized state and a liberal democracy; but chances are rather small in a country such as Albania, a relatively backward state with little former experience of a modern market economy and parliamentary democracy. All other East European states, including the European part of the former Soviet Union, fall somewhere between these two.

Consider in more detail the implications of the unspoken assumption "We can do it." What does it mean in practice relative to specific economic and political transformation? It means, among other things, that the accumulated experience and know-how of the West can be ignored by East Europeans in their pursuit of market economies and liberal democracies. However, rejection of the Western experience, deliberate or otherwise, bodes ill for Eastern Europe.

Most East Europeans have a poor perception, if any, of the link between private ownership and democracy. For many, there is no link. Some East Europeans even argue that one may achieve democracy without having private property and widespread dispersion of economic power. Historical evidence, however, does not support this view. Never in modern history has liberal democracy been achieved without the dispersion of economic power.

Furthermore, the importance of having a strong government able to cope with fundamental economic change is only vaguely understood by most East Europeans, including their politicians. That all East European states chose proportional electoral systems, often resulting in fragmented parliaments, evinces this clearly. In the case of Poland, the first free parliamentary election since the 1920s resulted in an extremely fragmented parliament with 29 parties represented in the Sejm (the lower house). This, in turn, led to weak governments based on coalitions of short duration. Between September 1989 and June 1993 Poland had four coalition governments, the last of these, the government of Hanna Suchocka, consisted of seven political parties and collapsed in a short time after losing a vote of confidence in the parliament.

Proportional electoral systems usually produce unstable political regimes unconducive to efficient economic transformation. What the domestic and international business community prefers is assurance, stability, and a set of clear rules regulating the market. This has been absent to a large degree in Eastern Europe. Likewise, a market economy may prosper if, *inter alia*, the underpinning legal system supports this kind of economy—where, for example, the rule of law prevails and promises are kept. Again, there is little evidence to prove that this is in fact the case in Eastern Europe today.[1]

Of equal importance with regard to fundamental political and economic change is the drastic transformation of Eastern European educational systems, stretching from crèche to university, including the mass media. A new political and business culture must be widely inculcated by educators from the onset of change. Yet nothing thus far indicates that many serious attempts have been undertaken in this regard. What must be achieved through the educational process in the region is, above all, a new understanding of what success is. When East Europeans are told that they have performed poorly in economics, sports, or some other field of activity, their typical answer is: "But we are not the worst one; behind us is Albania in Europe and Bangladesh in the world." What a strange perception of ambition and success, be it by an individual or by a group! For many an East European success is tantamount to not being last. Ambition is reduced to the unarticulated notion,"I shall be the second last." This, however, is the philosophy of a loser, not a winner. It is the worldview of one whose only ambition is to survive. Contrary to this attitude is the Western view: The sky is the limit—an attitude hardly known or practiced in Eastern Europe. Obviously, given the current Eastern European idea of success, prospects for change in the former communist states are fairly bleak.

Last, consider the role of the Christian Church in Eastern Europe. The Roman Catholic Church in particular appears not to give wholehearted countenance to the idea of a liberal democracy, capitalism, and a market economy. The same may be said of the Christian Orthodox Church in Russia and elsewhere in the region. Chances of successful economic and political transformation in Eastern Europe would increase considerably if both churches were to change their positions regarding wealth, trade, interest, and liberal and democratic values. In other words, the Catholic and Orthodox churches in Eastern Europe need to be more like the Protestant churches in the West.

All of the above shows that the Eastern European approach to fundamental change is indeed predicated on the largely false assumption "We can do it." But exactly why, when it comes to politics and economics, nations, societies, and even citizens nowadays think they "can do it" as well as the leading Western states is unclear.

Such a view was not the case before. It is a contemporary phenomenon, and it poses a serious hindrance to rapid and efficient transformation. It is said that about a thousand years ago, when the growing Russian state (Kievan Rus) became ungovernable, its rulers invited the Scandinavians to

take control of the country "because we don't know how to rule ourselves."
At issue is not whether this story is true but the attitude it demonstrates.
Closer to modern times, in the mid-nineteenth century a Russian tsar offered
a young German diplomat, Otto Von Bismarck, a high position in the
Russian foreign service. Such invitations and offers would simply be
unthinkable today.

This brings us to another phenomenon that needs to be mentioned here,
namely, nationalism. There is little doubt that nationalism bodes ill for
transformation in Eastern Europe. The assumption "we can do it" is based
largely on nationalistic feelings. The reason for this runs as follows: When
it comes to fundamental economic and political change, one cannot believe
and must not rely on foreigners because one cannot trust them. When taken
to extremes, this argument is fallacious. In practice, it may mean, and often
does mean, a search for new solutions, sometimes with disastrous results,
instead of adopting old, proven, and well-working devices, mechanisms,
and procedures in politics, economics, education or the legal system.

After all, when we look at something, we may not necessarily "see" it in
the same sense that a blind man "sees" when he says, "I see," meaning "I
understand." Most East Europeans look at the West and think that because
they "see" it, they also understand it. Not so. This is, in many cases, a
fundamental misconception. Humankind's social life is so complex, especially in the modern era, that very few people, if any, even in the West,
comprehend it entirely.

If Western economists fully understood how market economies operate,
then economic crises, unemployment, and inflation would never occur, or
would they? Yet, almost all economists in Eastern Europe believe they know
how to achieve stable market economies in their own country relatively
quickly.

Let me illustrate this with an example from the animal world. For many
years I used to visit a retired Australian farmer who had two dogs, which
he kept inside his house. The dogs discovered that in order to get out, they
had to push a fly-screen. They got out, but they never found out how to get
in. The farmer's daughter, who also had a dog, visited her father frequently,
along with her dog, which managed to enter the house from the outside by
pushing the door strongly. When the door swung open, the dog moved
forward quickly, whereupon the farmer's two dogs followed. Although the
two dogs did this hundreds of times, they never figured out how to get in
by themselves. They saw what happened but did not understand what they
saw. Something similar is observable in Eastern Europe, which watches the
West but often fails to comprehend the particular devices, solutions, and

mechanisms that have made the West economically powerful, with a relatively high standard of living for everyone, and politically stable.

Most of us learn through experience, not through reasoning alone, not through mere thinking. This is precisely what Eastern Europe lacks—experience. With the exception of the Czech Republic, Eastern Europe lacks the experience of market economies and liberal democracies. That does not mean, of course, that countries without experience of modern market economies and liberal democracies cannot become them now. Simply, doing so will not be easy, may take a long time, and quite likely will not be a goal achieved by all. It is the view of this author that the results for the region will most likely be mixed; we should expect the unexpected. Most of Eastern Europe has a rather strong tendency toward authoritarian rule. This tendency will be strengthened considerably by failure to deliver the economic goods quickly. Initially weak governments and fragmented parliaments may succumb to disorder and anarchy, and then to authoritarianism. Eventually there may appear a demagogue who will promise security and economic prosperity for all.

Since the fall of communism, Eastern Europe has undergone a revolution of raised expectations. If those expectations of a rosy future and a paradise on earth are not fulfilled soon, political instability in this part of the world will be the result, a consequence of the substantial loss of support for transformation into market economies and democracies.

Eastern Europe remains in a transitory phase that may last for another decade or so. The ultimate outcome of this is anybody's guess. That economic change in the former communist states is usually implemented by economists also bodes ill for the Eastern Europeans. Modern national economies are too complex to be transformed successfully by economists only, let alone by the former communist economists.

Most former communist economists simply do *not* understand how market economies operate, nor do they know the rules of the game. That they think they understand them makes things even worse, since to understand the nature of a problem means that the problem is already half solved.

When dealing with a fundamental transformation from one political system to another, that is, from communism to liberal democracy, *timeliness* is also of great importance. This too, it appears, is little understood by East European politicians. The goods must be delivered on short notice, otherwise disaffection will almost inevitably follow, with disastrous results for the region. Most likely some repercussions will be felt outside the region as well.

Another factor associated with the eventual success of political change in Eastern Europe, a factor widely discussed though little comprehended, is justice and fairness. Unlike their electorates, East European politicians by and large underestimate the importance of justice and fairness in their approach to transformation. To put it simply, most ordinary East Europeans who suffered under communist rule believe that today, under democratic rule, justice will prevail. Reality often refutes this. To give just one example, one of the best-known former East European dissidents, Adam Michnik, argues that "mercy should take place before justice" when dealing with former communist leaders. In practice, this statement means that mercy should replace justice, or to put it succinctly, "mercy instead of justice." Although it is ordinarily difficult to define justice, in a specific time and place we generally know reasonably well what justice is and we expect it to prevail. If however, this fails to happen, widespread disappointment and political apathy likely will occur, giving way to popular demagogues who will promise to punish the culprits. Such popular leaders would, in all likelihood, replace the nascent multiparty parliamentary democracies with authoritarian regimes based on arbitrary rule.

Usually, a swift fundamental change comes from the outside, for instance, when a military defeat in war is followed by a military occupation and the imposition by force of a new regime, as occurred after World War II. In recent history Germany and Japan are clear examples of the successful imposition by force of a new regime after defeat in war. Whereas immediately after the collapse of communism East Europeans appeared psychologically prepared and willing to accept fundamental change, many of their politicians were not.

This brings us to the next factor relevant to the prospects for drastic change in Eastern Europe, namely, vested interests. Because communism collapsed in Eastern Europe almost entirely as a result of internal causes and not outside ones, numerous people there continue to have vested interests and enough power to defend them, reserving as much as possible of the state-run economy and other entrenched institutions. Experience shows that in peaceful times it is often extremely difficult to implement thorough fundamental transformation. Clearly much is at stake, and potential losers will defend their perceived interests as forcefully as they can under the circumstances.

Another obstacle to rapid transition from a command economy to a market one is a peculiar approach to profit making in some parts of Eastern Europe. Broadly speaking, there are two, very different approaches: One we can label as the French one, the other as the Chinese. Not much research and observation are required to notice that in big Western cities there are many more Chinese restaurants than French ones. If we assume that for foreigners both cuisines are equally tasty, then, we may also assume that the answer to why there are more Chinese restaurants in New York, Melbourne, or London is related to the price. The French people usually sell a small meal for a high price. The Chinese do just the opposite: They sell large meals, cheaply.

What are the practical implications for an individual business, an employee, and the national economy of these dramatically different approaches to profit making? In the French case, few people would be employed in restaurants because of high prices and low demand for French food. Of course, the opposite holds true in the Chinese case. Furthermore, a big demand for Chinese food would have a spillover effect, leading to a higher demand for agricultural products, real estate, transport, and so on.

Now, if in a given country the Chinese way of making money is adopted in most spheres of economic activity, ultimately, all other things being equal, this would lead to a higher standard of living for the population as a whole. Why? Because when consumer goods and services are sold at low prices, consumers can buy more for the same amount of money. If they buy more, production increases. And when production goes up, two beneficial effects follow: Economy of scale allows manufactured goods to be sold even more cheaply, and the number of employed people increases. Now there is more money in circulation; hence, as the demand for goods and services increases, so does the supply. Clearly the Chinese approach to profit making is an engine of economic growth for the national economy and, sometimes, may lead to economic development.

What is meant by economic development here is economic growth that eventually results in a higher standard of living for an entire society. To experience economic development, it seems, a deliberate government policy to this effect is required. In other words, economic development is a result of a conscious *political* decision. One glance at Eastern Europe is sufficient to conclude that to its peoples, the Chinese approach to profit making is almost totally alien. For some, even the French approach to profit is unsatisfactory. The ideal business transaction for many Eastern Europeans is to sell a product or service at a profit high enough to enable the sellers to retire immediately and live in comfort for the rest of their lives.

East European observers argue that to sustain and consolidate systemic changes is even more difficult than to initiate them. If this view is correct, then additional measures to diminish the risk of failure must be ensured. One key measure would be an institution for economic transformation independent of government. Such an institution would need to be independent to lessen the political pressure on the people implementing these changes, for initially most people will have their standard of living lowered, and their discontent will produce political pressure either to stop the transformations altogether or at least to slow down the pace of change. However, any delay in the pace of change carries with it an increasing risk of failure. Therefore economic transformations should be rapid and comprehensive enough to create large constituencies whose interest in a market economy surpasses their interest in favoring past communist regimes. Thus far only the Germans, and perhaps the Czechs, have managed this.

In addition, devolution of political authority—for instance in the form of a federation—will significantly diminish the risk of failure, as it stimulates both political competition and economic competition within federated states while, at the same time, limiting mistakes. It also brings politics closer to the people, making government more comprehensible to ordinary citizens as well as giving them more to say on issues that affect them. Consequently, the number of people interested in supporting the new democratic regime should grow. A federation, by definition, denotes dispersion of political and economic power, and this, too, gives better prospects for democracy to survive than would be the case in a unitary state.

Obviously, with regard to the development of entrepreneurial skills, new private businesses are more important than privatized ones. Yet many private medium-sized businesses were formerly state owned, and many large businesses in Eastern Europe today are still state run.

Since systemic change affects practically everybody, a consensus not only on goals but also on means is highly desired. Credibility and confidence in blueprints for change and individuals who implement them are very important. Inconsistency and vacillation of politicians usually generate distrust and cynicism among the people.

From what has been said thus far, it follows that to succeed quickly in transforming communism to a democracy requires resoluteness and a clear vision of *what* to do and *how* to do it. But this is not enough. Also, to ensure success in Eastern Europe, a new approach to transformation is needed—a rapid, *total* change based on justice and fairness and heavy reliance on Western experience. It is the argument of this book that systemic change demands no less than such "new totalism." It is unlikely that "muddling through" will work in this case.

The next chapter discusses systemic change in Eastern Europe since the collapse of communism. Then presented in Chapters 3, 4, and 5 are detailed analyses of the changes in Russia, Poland, and the Czech Republic, respectively. Chapter 6 deals with Western aid to postcommunist Eastern Europe.

Finally, the concluding chapter considers the progress made thus far toward a liberal democracy and a market economy; it also assesses Eastern Europe's prospects for enduring success in this regard.

NOTE

This introduction is adapted from my chapter in the volume *The Loss of Innocence: International Relations Essays in Honour of Dirk Kunert*, edited by Colin Vale and Irene van den Ende. Johannesburg: Human Sciences Research Council, 1994.

1. Carsten Hermann-Pilath, "Systemic Transformation as an Economic Problem," *Aussen Politik*, Vol. 42, No. 2, 1992, pp. 171–182.

2 Eastern Europe After the Collapse of Communism

The sudden though expected fall of communism in Eastern Europe and the Soviet Union had much more to do with the Soviet leaders' loss of faith in communism as a superior system to capitalism than their countries' poor performance in economics, science, and the arms race. Almost from the onset of the communist era, unbiased observers saw clearly that the new system based on a state-owned economy (private property was abolished nearly overnight) was no match to systems grounded on private property and competition. Especially the lack of the latter, competition, resulted after a while in shrinking national economies and declining standards of living in all communist states.

Initially Soviet leaders explained away the poor economic performance of their country by pointing to its backwardness and, later, to the destruction of the Soviet economy during World War II. As time passed, however, evidence mounted in support of the old observation that systems devoid of competition perform worse than those that are based on it. Czechoslovakia, for instance, was an industrialized country that had had a relatively high standard of living between the two world wars, yet after the imposition of communism its national economy, not destroyed by the war, eventually stagnated. East Germany, also an industrialized state, evinced similar results, as did other Eastern European states, with even much worse economic results.

As we know, empires declining economically and militarily may last for many centuries before they eventually collapse. The almost simultaneous collapse of both communism and the Soviet empire toward the end of the twentieth century was not inevitable at this particular time; certainly the system could have lasted while decaying for many more years if not centuries. That it fell when it did without an outside cause, such as defeat in a war, must be attributed to the Moscow leaders' disenchantment with communism. Undoubtedly Gorbachev, unlike Khrushchev, never, as the Soviet ruler, thought communism would "catch up and overtake" capitalism in economic productivity and standards of living. In other words, the last communist leadership in the Soviet Union went through a revolutionary change of mind. "The most important of all revolutions is," as Edmund Burke aptly noted two centuries ago, "a revolution in sentiments, manners and moral opinions."[1] And this is exactly what happened in the Soviet Union after over seventy years of experience with communism.

Disappointed with communism and economically burdened to run the largest empire that ever existed, Soviet rulers granted East European states independence, which in turn resulted in a breakup of the Soviet Union itself. When communism fell nearly everybody thought that once democracy and capitalism replaced the old system, prosperity for all would materialize nearly overnight. The example of prosperous neighboring Western European democratic and capitalist states and the United States was perhaps the single most important reason why the East Europeans opted for political pluralism and a market economy.

For a few years after 1989 Eastern Europeans went through a revolution of rising expectations certain that now a high standard of living comparable to that of the Western societies would soon be achieved relatively easily. In the decade since then that dream has not been realized even in the former East Germany, now united with West Germany, let alone in other former communist states, which received much less Western aid and expertise than East Germany.[2]

Despite an economy that since 1992 has grown between 7 and 10 percent per year, "making [the former East Germany] the fastest growing region in Europe," in 1994 East Germans cast almost one in every five votes in local state and federal elections in favor of the communist party.[3] Little wonder that other East Europeans are at least equally disillusioned with the pace of economic change. As it turns out, the demise of a command economy does not by itself always result in a higher standard of living for all. In fact, some segments of society in every country of the region have suffered a decline in their standard of living since then. This surprising outcome has brought about unexpected changes of government: in four East European states former communist parties returned to power; this time they got to power peacefully through a democratic ballot.[4] That single occurrence demonstrates vividly how deep and widespread disaffection with postcommunist reality is in certain parts, perhaps most parts, of Eastern Europe.[5]

A question arises here: What went wrong? Cannot the East Europeans cope with democracy and capitalism? Perhaps the communist system was not so bad after all, since people voluntarily returned power to the former communists. (In some countries, such as Serbia, for instance, the communists have not yet lost power.)

To say, however, that the former communists came back to power in many countries of the region does not mean that they did it in all countries. The Czech Republic especially is the "odd man out" in the region in the sense that not only has a postcommunist party not regained power there but also never thus far has any leftist party ruled the country, alone or in coalition, since the collapse of communism in late 1989. Admittedly, many Czechs proudly point out that since the peaceful or "velvet" revolution, the country has been ruled uninterruptedly by center-right coalition governments, the only such ones in the entire region still surviving by the late 1990s.[6]

Why is the postcommunist systemic change in the Czech Republic different from that in the rest of Eastern Europe? Do the country's present achievements have to do with its current way of dealing with fundamental transformation, or do they relate to its precommunist past? Or perhaps to both? These questions on the Czech case certainly merit attention and will be discussed in detail in a later chapter. For now, let us examine the general systemic change that occurred in Eastern Europe since 1989.

It is the argument of this chapter that the past matters strongly in relation to the present transformation of postcommunist societies and its ultimate outcome in the foreseeable future. This is not to say, however, that the future is preordained and that we can do nothing about it. On the contrary, we are the masters of our destiny; yet the past exerts a stronger impact in the short run than in the long run—and this, in the case of societies, may mean several generations if not centuries. For this reason, an abrupt change in a given society in its modus operandi, and the different results brought about by it, occurs rarely and is usually caused by force from without. Such is the power of the past that traditional behaviors, customs, and ways of thinking sometimes survive over millennia.[7] Yet because in the very long run everything changes, this region is not, as some people claim, "imprisoned by its own history."[8]

The view of the present author is that to know the past helps us to understand the present and to predict the near future. A well-known nineteenth-century political philosopher argued that "the entire man is, so to speak, to be seen in the cradle of the child. The growth of nations presents something analogous to this; they all bear some marks of their origin. The circumstances which accompanied their birth and contributed to their development affect the whole term of their being."[9]

With regard to Eastern Europe as a region, its political and economic development since at least the Renaissance has been and remains different from that of the West. Since the sixteenth century Eastern Europe has been an economically underdeveloped and marginalized part of Europe.[10] When modern democracy emerged in the West in the second half of the nineteenth and early twentieth centuries, Eastern Europe did not follow suit. Between World War I and World War II democracy prevailed only in Czechoslovakia; in all other states dictatorial rule quickly replaced fragile democratic regimes. In the aftermath of the last world war communism was imposed, usually by force, in the entire region. That means that in Eastern Europe capitalism has never fully developed and markets, though not totally absent, were deficient.[11] As a result of long communist rule, nearly half a century in Eastern Europe, and over seventy years in the Soviet Union, the region's economic backwardness and marginalization has increased, reaching its peak at the time of the collapse of communism.

Given the above, it follows that modern capitalism founded on a market economy and liberal democracy are not going to be brought back or reinstated but introduced, virtually for the first time.[12] Can market institutions and culture, liberal attitudes and democratic behavior, be decreed into existence a day after the departure of communism? Or is time, and a lot of it, required? In Russia, communism lasted for approximately three generations, which means there are no people in that country who have memories and experience of another political and social system, which might serve as a guide to current politics and economics. In this respect in other countries of the region the situation is better, since communism there lasted for about two generations, which means that old generations there were brought up in and experienced a life very different from that after the year 1945. This gives Eastern Europe some advantage over Russia in relation to a potentially better economic performance in the near future, but only just that.

What counts more than that, however, are individuals' decisions, governments' actions, and states' politics after the relinquishment of communism. Despite the arguments of some scholars, the end of the Cold War has not by itself "dissolved an artificial region," Eastern Europe.[13] The region remains; it was never "artificial." Still, some of its inhabitants now prefer to call themselves "Central Europeans," hoping, perhaps, that a mere name change will somehow bring them closer to the West. To be called "West

European" is undoubtedly their ultimate goal. Will they or some of them really achieve it, say, within a generation or two? It depends. It depends on the decisions made today in the realms of economics, politics, education, and law, in particular.

With regard to fundamental, systemic change—that is to say, a movement from one regime to another, drastically different regime—the appropriate question to ask is, "*How* to do it?" Much depends on the answer, and equally much depends on implementation of the answer; words alone will not do the trick, however correct they may be. For clarity, the above question is divided into several, more specific ones dealing with the scope, pace, and sequencing of the systemic change as well as the exercise of justice.[14] These questions seem to be the most crucial ones, though by no means the only ones to be asked. Additional questions, more detailed in character, are tackled later in the chapter, and the highly disputed Western aid to Eastern Europe is discussed in a separate chapter.

Rephrasing the question regarding the scope of systemic change, we can ask, "*What* to change?" In all likelihood answering will be easier when the question is put thus. The question might be even easier to answer if one ponders what *not* to change, that is, what from communism is worthwhile preserving. Has communism produced anything that ought to be saved because it worked so well, producing great results, or was so more efficient than its counterpart in the West, whether in the sphere of economics, politics, social life, science, the military, or ecology? If upon consideration one concludes that virtually nothing from the old regime was really worth preserving, then obviously the systemic transformation must be comprehensive. Because the question about the scope of change refers to values, one cannot prove that someone's views are either right or wrong; one's choice of values, one's point of view, is restricted only by one's experience, imagination, and vision of what makes human life great.

In real life people are almost always divided when it comes to choice, preferences, and values. This case is, of course, no different. Broadly speaking, three views concerning the scope of systemic transformation have emerged since 1989: On the one hand are adherents of the communist system who want to save as much as possible of the old regime; on the other hand are proponents of a thorough, deep, and comprehensive change. Between these groups are advocates of a middle road, or a "third road" after the demise of communism; that is, they are people without liberal views who in the realm of economy want to preserve the state's decisive role through a variety of means.

Unconditional defenders of the communist past are few nowadays and pose a negligible political force anywhere in Eastern Europe or the former Soviet Union. The really important struggle is that between supporters of a comprehensive, total change and adherents of a piecemeal, partial change who, in other words, wish to combine elements of communism and elements of capitalism in the economy, politics, and other spheres of national life. Most likely, the outcome of that struggle will determine the future of Eastern Europe for many generations to come.

It seems that at the time of this writing, people who opt for a "third road" are on the ascent, which was not the case immediately after the collapse of communism when a rosy future seemed just around the corner. But because that dream about prosperity did not materialize quickly, as unrealistically expected, and in fact the standards of living of many people fell, in increasing numbers the voters started backing a variety of political parties that, to put it mildly, dislike a market economy, free international trade, and liberal, democratic values.

At the beginning of economic change in Eastern Europe observers noted that change exacts severe costs immediately and this is certain, whereas after a while it may produce benefits, and this is uncertain. Primarily for this reason many people in the former Soviet empire today are inclined to countenance parties that are not for an outright liberal democracy and free market but opt for limited domestic competition and protection of the national economy against international competition as well as restricted or partial privatization. They argue that the social costs of transition are likely to be lowest under a limited transformation program.

One proponent of the "third road" goes as far as to argue for "market socialism" by which he means a self-managed socialist model where firms are owned by their employees. In his view, this "can be a viable economic system and a possible alternative to capitalism."[15]

Among persons who benefited from privatization are many members of the former *nomenklatura*, that is, people who occupied top communist party positions. This well known fact is used to argue against further privatization on the grounds that it benefits people who deserve punishment rather than awards. It has also been observed that the market awards persons with business acumen, and because most people lack business know-how, they often envy those who have it and succeed. Unemployment, unknown under the old regime but widespread today, is also used as an argument against drastic change and thoroughgoing privatization. That there was no unemployment during communist rule supposedly reveals the superiority of the communist system over one based on private property and competition.

Not all who defend partial, limited transformation do so for altruistic reasons, however, wishing to help those who suffer during change. More often than not, all those who can gain by market imperfection, protectionism, and monopolies, to name a few, will demand a stop to the transformation. This is, for obvious reasons, understandable and expected. Actually, one could argue that one of the "iron laws" of fundamental change is that it produces resistance to it proportional to the strength and pace of it; as one shrewd observer put it, "[The] reform process itself generates incentives to stop halfway."[16]

Five years after economic change began in Russia about half of the country's people described their lives as "unbearable" and began losing faith in a market economy and in democracy.[17] Notwithstanding this change of opinion, to achieve the goals of widespread prosperity and a stable democracy, persevering in policies necessary to bring about complete transformation is the key to success.[18] Otherwise, what threatens Eastern Europe, according to Bulgarian president Zhelyu Zhelev, is not the return of communism but "the ossification of postcommunism," or only a partially transformed communism.[19]

Fundamental economic change in Eastern Europe has resulted in lower standards of living for many people. Society may not continue to accept deterioration of its living conditions and thus reject this change through the voting ballot. Hence, it is argued, initial transformation should have a limited character, comprising only the economy and leaving political change from dictatorial rule to democracy to a later stage. A strong government, not subject to the threat of losing power through periodic elections, would more easily carry on with the painful economic transformation, it is maintained, bringing it to a successful end, than would a weak government fighting for its political life.[20] Although this argument sounds plausible, is it accurate and supported by empirical evidence? Proponents point to the example of several Southeast Asian undemocratic regimes that have successfully led their societies from poverty to a relatively high standard of living in recent decades.

Observers frequently assume that East Europeans prefer democracy to any other kind of government for its own sake and not just because it is associated today with the welfare state and a high standard of living. But what to do if this is not the case? "Should we force democracy on people who may not be able to handle it and destroy stability?" asked the Malaysian prime minister.[21] "In a number of East Asian countries," he stated, "while democracy is still eschewed, the free market has been accepted and has brought prosperity. Perhaps it is the authoritarian stability which enabled this to happen."[22]

Furthermore, observers also assert that fragile and weak democracies cannot enforce attempted changes or the law that protects ordinary citizens; hence this will pose an additional impediment to a successful transformation. Under dictatorial rule these obstacles either do not exist or are ignored, making the chances of succeeding in one's effort much greater. If it is true that most people will accept a fair amount of hardship for a while but have limited patience, then to proceed with economic change in the face of mounting difficulties and people's growing impatience is, according to some observers, easier under a nondemocratic regime.[23]

For a variety of reasons relating to cost, ideology, and tradition some people argue that certain areas of public life, for instance, education, health, and agriculture, should be excluded from transformation, at least initially. In Russia, a country that has for decades been unable to feed itself as a result of low productivity caused by the forcible nationalization of its arable lands, agriculture has not yet undergone meaningful change. The reasons transformation should be restricted in scope seem endless and growing. For example, many in Eastern Europe still argue that state-owned property—that is, nearly all state-owned property—should not be privatized in its entirety, especially large industry, some transport, communication, certain mass media, education, and the military. Frequently selling large enterprises to domestic buyers is difficult only because local businesspeople are short of large capital, and yet the idea of selling to foreign buyers often evokes strong and effective protests just because the purchaser is alien. Foreign capital activity, it is claimed, is detrimental to a host country; if so, the corollary is that it is better to limit the scope of transformation by preserving some state-owned companies rather than selling them to overseas buyers. Doing so is an exercise in damage control, a way to limit detrimental activity, or a lesser evil, according to its proponents.

The above arguments in favor of limited transformation, though powerful, are by no means comprehensive. Arguments in favor of total transformation are fewer and, perhaps at first glance, less convincing to an unbiased reader than arguments favoring limited change. But whether total change is, indeed, less effective is a different matter altogether.

Proponents of a comprehensive, systemic change by definition opt for a systemic change comprising the entire public life, politics, and economics; that is, they prefer total to partial transformation for pragmatic or ideological reasons and sometimes for a combination of reasons. In this respect they do not differ from their opponents. This, however, is not the point. The point is, Who is right and who is not? In other words, which of the two approaches to fundamental change is more effective, and which has the bigger chance for success?

Many people throughout the world prefer democracy for its own sake regardless of its link to the economy. Such was the case from ancient times until the nineteenth century. Preference for a political system without prejudice to economic well-being is a value judgment and as such cannot be disputed. Today, however, there are also a great number of people who prefer democracy because of its apparent link to the economy, specifically, through the welfare state and through high standards of living. This is a new phenomenon at present widely observed in Eastern Europe, seen especially in the first months after the collapse of communism. Holders of this view maintain that postcommunist transformation *must* be comprehensive in scope because democracy somehow ensures economic prosperity. To substantiate their claim, they point to the West: All contemporary Western societies are both democratic and affluent. In addition, in the world today in no democratic liberal state do the majority of people live in poverty. Does this example not show that in our times democracy generates wealth and abundance for the people who practice it?

Indeed, plenty of scholars, politicians, and ordinary people in both the West and the East think so. They assert, "However we look at it, a comprehensive transition appears more beneficial" than one limited in scope.[24] The most crucial and least discussed issue, however, is whether one can accomplish democracy without fundamental economic transformation. To put it differently, is democracy attainable under a communist economy, that is, where private ownership is drastically limited and the national economy is run by monopolies—in an economy where, by definition, competition is absent and so is a market economy, which is based upon it.

Supporters of comprehensive change argue that the goal of a durable democracy is unattainable unless the state economic monopoly is destroyed. Otherwise, so the argument goes, the state as an employer, and the only employer in the country, has too much power. Hence the temptation to abolish the nascent democracy is too strong to resist; and because of an enormous accumulation of political and economic power, this is relatively easy to achieve. One may ask why the state should, as a rule, relinquish democracy, given the circumstances described above. The answer is that democracy is perceived by some as an impediment to the smooth running of a country whereas the opposite holds true in relation to nondemocratic regimes. The corollary is that "for the good of the people" democracy ought to be supplemented by dictatorial rule; only then will wealth be created swiftly, the economy prosper, and the people be happy.

Dispersion of economic power is, however, a necessary condition for the establishment of lasting democracy.[25] The more widely economic power is dispersed, the better the prospects are for democracy. It follows that to enhance the democratic regime, ideally there should be few, if any, state-owned firms because they grossly narrow the state's power. In further defense of comprehensive change, advocates point to the fact that never in modern times has democracy existed without private property and the dispersion of economic power. In addition, they maintain, in a situation where the national economy is based on a few monopolies, even if privately owned, the chances for democracy to survive in the long run are negligible. Why? The evidence given is empirical: When the state faces organized or poorly organized labor, it usually supports business interest over the people's interests because, among other things, it benefits from the arrangement. After all, what are the benefits for the ruling elite to support the people's interests? To give a convincing answer to that question is rather difficult, is it not?

A decrease in state economic power is best achieved through widespread and thorough privatization; this means fragmentation of economic power among many people with different, often clashing interests and, at the same stroke, a boost in economic efficiency and productivity.[26] The latter, in turn, it is claimed, consolidates the nascent weak and fragile democracy. With growing wealth and abundance, it seems, democracy becomes more attractive to the people, and this is what matters here.

To further entrench the new democracy, doing away with the state economic monopoly is not enough; much more must be done to secure success. Above all, the state monopoly of information must be broken; contemporary democracy is unimaginable without the free flow of uncensored news and information. It follows that also in the mass media, widely dispersed ownership, preferably mainly private, is most conducive to a sustainable democracy.

Additionally, cogent argument in support of comprehensive economic change, through privatization in particular, relates to people's pains and hardships suffered after the collapse of communism. If the process of privatization stops somewhere midway, it is argued, then people disillusioned with the economic results brought by it will vote into office politicians who will end the transformation for good. Only comprehensive privatization will eliminate those forces that have interests in preserving as many state-owned firms as possible. If this fails to occur, democracy is at stake. Political parties inimical to a market economy might come to power, and they would not only stop or greatly slow down economic change but also weaken the fragile democracies. For stopping or slowing down fundamental economic change will result in *prolonging* the low and declining standards of living of many people, thus almost inevitably increasing the numbers of those disaffected with democracy. Evidence? Several years after the demise of communism four former communist parties returned to power in as many countries due to widespread voter disenchantment with high prices and inflation, growing unemployment, crime, and corruption. These problems are predominantly economic in nature.

Although a decline in the general standard of living seems unavoidable, whether under a comprehensive transformation or a less drastic one, "the social costs of transition," argue the advocates of thorough change, "are likely to be lowest under a radical reform scenario."[27] Furthermore, the mistakes of the radicals can be corrected, whereas those of their opponents can be fatal to the new regime, possibly blocking the transformation or even creating a system unexpected and unwanted by the electorate and themselves.[28] So though a return to the status quo ante, that is, to communism, is anticipated by virtually no one, a Third World status for Eastern Europe is predicted by some observers. "I see no reason," stated a renowned expert on transformation, "why the future of Czechoslovakia should be different from that of Argentina, Brazil or Chile."[29] If the final outcome of the systemic change in Eastern Europe "is to be a form of capitalism, it is unlikely to be the sort of capitalism we know in Western Europe and North America," declared another.[30]

Thorough privatization is also defended on grounds of efficiency. According to Nobel Prize laureate in economics Milton Friedman, "Nobody spends other people's money as cautiously and prudently as his own."[31] This suggests that to avoid waste of capital, private ownership is superior to any other system of ownership. Time and again this has been confirmed by the performance of national economies based predominantly on private property compared with those economies that have abolished private ownership, namely command or communist economies. But this is not enough; private ownership of business by itself does not necessarily lead to efficient allocation of resources unless the national economy is based on competition as well. Proof? In many Third World countries in Latin America, Asia, and Africa, large parts of the national economy are privately owned but little, if any, competition exists there. The result is high prices, low-quality goods and services, and because of this a low standard of living if not outright poverty for the majority and riches for just the few. It has been observed time and again that where there is no incentive to produce high-quality goods cheaply, this does not happen, because commodities will be sold regardless of quality and price in an environment where consumers have no choice but to buy what is available.

Lack of competition creates a *producers' market*, whereas a competitive economy creates a *buyers'* or *consumers' market,* meaning that purchasers have a choice of products to buy and they will buy goods that are cheap and of high quality too. For producers to survive, let alone to prosper, they must deliver to the market commodities of top quality and low price, otherwise they may go bankrupt. In an economy operating competitively the consumer is the ultimate winner, getting more products for less money than they would cost elsewhere. This means that the consumer saves more money than would be the case under the opposite conditions. When consumers save more money, they may spend it on other, additional products or services, thus creating a higher demand. Higher demand, in turn, leads to bigger production and employment, putting more money in circulation, which, again, may be spent, and so on. . . . This is the way, argue the advocates of competition, to move from poverty to riches, to create wealth for the many not just the few, the latter being the history of humankind until recent times. From what has been said thus far, it follows that for East Europeans to prosper economically, they must avoid state and private monopolies,[32] as well as mixed economies, that is, economies based on both private property and state ownership.[33] Certainly the perfect market economy has never existed, and neither has a perfect command economy; real-life economies are a mixture of both. But the proportions do matter and do make a difference, the difference being either to live in poverty or in abundance.

Many adherents of systemic-wide economic transformation also strongly support a fundamental political change from communism to democracy not only because of their dislike of dictatorships as such but also because of democracy's intrinsic qualities as a device for change, including economic change. They maintain that democracy, better than any other political system, allows implementation of drastic change, although perhaps it does not introduce it. As one adherent put it: "Democracy as a mechanism for economic adjustment offers advantages over dictatorships. Elections install new governments that can draw support from new constituencies and claim mandates for reform; they also can blame the outgoing incumbents for the crises necessitating adjustment."[34] Some empirical evidence suggests that "under democracy there is more scope for support of painful reforms as well as more rational bases for resistance to reforms than is frequently acknowledged."[35] No wonder nowadays it is claimed that "the fate of democracy becomes intertwined with economic performance."[36]

This being so, people's attitudes toward, opinions of, and sentiments about the yet largely unknown market system and democracy in general must become positive and their expectations must be kept low in order to enhance the chances for successful fundamental transformation. Long ago it was noted that people's

> sentiments can not be directly detected. Opinions and actions are the empirical manifestations of sentiments, and only these manifestations can be directly observed. Even a very superficial view of present society reveals streams of opinion that manifest underlying sentiments and interests are the forces at work determining the character of social equilibrium.[37]

Several years after the collapse of communism people's opinions of, and sentiments toward, the new order are increasingly less favorable if not outwardly hostile. To modify those feelings, however, not only economic success but radical transformation of the entire education system is required. Systemic change cannot be narrowed to economics and politics only. Yet rarely is the topic of education mentioned in connection with economic and political change in Eastern Europe. This is a strange situation because "the struggles that will help determine the fate of liberal democracy . . . will occur at the levels of civil society and culture. The realms [are] crucial for new democracies emerging from an authoritarian past."[38] Some people argue that a profoundly antidemocratic culture would impede the spread of democratic values in the society, and deny legitimacy to democratic institutions, thus weakening the forces that work toward the consolidation of democracy. Some critics even go so far as to contend that for historical reasons democracy is largely inappropriate for non-Western societies, and that, we must assume, refers to most parts of Eastern Europe.[39]

One means of changing East European culture, values, and behavior is undoubtedly through education, which itself requires change, primarily what is taught and how it is taught. Yet politicians in that part of Europe give education little attention and low priority. Expenditures on education have declined since 1989. The return of former communists to power in some countries has led to suppression of school autonomy and parental control.[40]

The most important thing to change in education is the method of teaching social science and the humanities. The East European method of teaching is based on the principal that there is only one truth, and that truth is known to the teacher, who passes it on to his or her pupils.The students' task is to learn that "truth" by rote and recite it back to the teacher, proving thereby that they have learned it. This approach, grounded on one unquestionable truth, has existed in Eastern Europe since at least the Middle Ages, only to be boosted to higher levels by Marxist-Leninist regimes in recent times. Such uncritical absorption of knowledge is inimical to liberal democratic values of tolerance, compromise, and minority rights.

To compromise, to meet another person midway, is perceived in Eastern Europe as a defeat. To a person of honor, in a no-win situation death is preferable to compromise, since to give up even a bit to save the rest is regarded as surrender, and what can be worse than that? Compromise lies at the heart of liberal democracy. Without compromise, democracy is unthinkable: In a system where diverse values and interests are acknowledged, solution to a conflict is usually achieved through accommodation. This fosters tolerance toward other people's ideas, opinions, and interests, and tolerance in practice denotes that minority rights are protected, even cherished, by the majority, for one day the majority may become a minority. It follows that liberal democracy nurtures relativism, that is, relative values as opposed to the absolute values so popular in Eastern Europe and so vigorously propagated there by the Roman Catholic Church. A society whose culture is firmly entrenched in absolute values, propagated by the educational system, has little chance of successful transformation from communism to democracy and a market economy unless the change encompasses the values themselves. This amounts to no less than a revolution in basic ideas, or values, and consequently in political and economic behavior.

Can a revolution of ideas be achieved in a short span of time? The demise of communism did not create a systemic vacuum to be filled at will "with a new system."[41] To change overnight people's way of thinking and acting seems difficult indeed, if not impossible, and *who* is going to do it? Former communist educators are by definition the worst equipped for the task. Are former political dissidents turned politicians in several countries better prepared for this? They were born and brought up in communist states, they grew up with little knowledge, not to mention experience, of life in the West.

Yet optimists contend that this can be achieved through learning from others. If so, then we must ask whether the East Europeans want to learn from others. Do they, for instance, want to learn from émigrés who have returned to their native countries in recent years? Available evidence shows that this not to be the case. Former émigrés, overall, perform poorly in public life, in politics in particular. "Strong émigré personalities are perceived as alien by the majority of the electorate. The popular perception of diasporas is a combination of mistrust, envy and fear. [This attitude] drastically limits the diaspora's impact during the transition from communism."[42] If the East Europeans usually mistrust their former émigrés, do they trust strangers, people of the West, who are experts or specialists in a certain area? The answer is that this depends on the area of expertise. Broadly speaking, people with know-how in science, medicine, engineering, and especially the military are trusted and their advice sought and appreciated. The opposite holds true with regard to politics, economics, education, and law.

When an Eastern European leader is seriously ill Western doctors are generally consulted and often the life of those leaders lies in their hands.[43] In matters of less serious consequence for political leaders, strange as it may sound, foreigners are not trusted, let alone asked to become decision makers in their respective field of expertise, especially if their fields are politics or economics. But politics and economics by their very nature are less of a science than, say, medicine, and more of an art, which means that in this area a mixture of experience, insight, and shrewdness, particularly concerning democracy and market economies, is very important—and precisely because of that all but nonexistent in Eastern Europe. To reiterate, under the communists it was relatively easy to produce world-class mathematicians but nearly impossible to do the same in the realm of the social sciences, for example, in economics. Yet what the East Europeans need most since the collapse of communism is a thorough Western "brainwashing" in public life and the social sciences. "Without the help of the social sciences," contend some scholars, "the transformation [in Eastern Europe] is doomed to failure."[44]

It has been confirmed time and again that changing people's customs and habits is extremely difficult especially in the short-run, and that occurs rarely. "Such is the influence of custom," argued an eighteenth-century philosopher, "that where it is strongest it not only covers our natural ignorance but even conceals itself, and seems not to take place, merely because it is found in the highest degree."[45] Many years of communist rule notwithstanding, it has been noticed with surprise that "the nascent party systems of Central and Eastern Europe bear striking resemblance to those of the interwar years, almost as if the region had awoken in 1990 from a deep sleep of more than half a century."[46]

Several East European states now wish to join the North Atlantic Treaty Organization (NATO), the Western military alliance. In the opinion of NATO officials the communist era "mentality," not the lack of expensive Western hardware, is the greatest impediment to joining the alliance. "To change the cultural attitude of the military leaders is the most difficult challenge in these countries," declared a NATO military attaché.[47] To change the politicians', economists', and educators' modes of thinking and acting will be no easier, however, if anything, it will be even more difficult to achieve, because the habits of the military are more technical in nature than the habits of the general public. More important, soldiers in the East and in the West have more in common, one would expect, than civilians in these two regions. "Why does the domain of culture show such persistence, why are strong habits, accustomed codes, mental frames so hard to unlearn, to eradicate and to dismantle?" asked a puzzled East European scholar.[48]

To make democracy work seems to require a certain degree of political competence on the part of a nation's citizens and, especially, elected leaders. For this reason in nascent democracies the question of citizen competence possesses an obvious urgency.[49] Do the Europeans have sufficient competence to turn their newly democratizing states into a lasting success? Obviously the values nurtured under the communist regime must be replaced by an altogether different set of rules and civic virtues needed in a capitalist liberal democracy. Each system generates its own characteristic features that makes it viable and enduring. For instance, when feudal order was superseded by capitalism, a total revolution in the organization of society, the economy, law, science, religion, and the arts occurred.

Max Weber, in his seminal book *The Protestant Ethic and the Spirit of Capitalism*, asked a pertinent question concerning what caused the replacement of feudalism with capitalism. His answer was that for capitalism to emerge, a certain type of personality was needed, one that would fit the competitive, enterprising spirit of the new order, that is, personality based on the Protestant ethic which produced the hard working, disciplined, methodical individual. In economics the rational ethics of ascetic Protestantism superseded the Catholic ethic of a fixed order based on the medieval doctrine of the just price and the just wage.[50]

Since Eastern Europe is now moving toward capitalism and democracy, one wonders to what extent the enterprising personality and democratic character is encountered in that region. It seems not to a great extent, due to its past; that is not to argue, however, that at present Eastern Europeans are not undergoing a revolutionary change of ideas, customs, and modes of acting. How widespread and long-lasting the process is, is difficult to judge, and its ultimate outcome remains to be seen. The fact is that the communist regimes ill prepared people for life in a society where the economy and politics are based on competition. Competition demands efficiency, hard work, risk, and imagination—characteristics rare under the old regime, which instead fostered obedience, hypocrisy, and mediocrity. These features totally deny those cherished in the West. Although Eastern Europe was not communist before World War II, little there smacked of capitalism and even less of democracy. One could thus contend that as far as the individual's personality is concerned, the change to communism was perhaps easier to make than a move in the opposite direction, from communism to a democracy and capitalism. It follows that Eastern Europe suffers from a deficit of Western values. It took centuries for the West to achieve what it possesses now. Should it take less time for the East? Are shortcuts possible?

Certainly, to know in advance where one is heading may help, but that in itself does not guarantee that one will get to the target. Furthermore, can one build a new order and at the same time establish certain civic virtues that are indispensable to it? Pointing to historical evidence, some people argue that this is unlikely. In the United States, "civil society was first, and the state came later. Switzerland is even today more a civil society, than a state."[51]

Admittedly, what greatly facilitates fundamental change is political stability, so politicians and citizens alike can focus more of their attention on the process of systemic change instead of, say, industrial strikes or too frequent general elections. Obviously, the electoral system is intertwined with political stability or lack of it. It was observed long ago that an electoral system based on proportional representation often leads to short-lived coalition governments and frequent elections. A good example in Western Europe is Italy, which has had fifty governments in as many years since the end of World War II. Despite the evidence, once communism fell in Eastern Europe all the states of the region opted for proportional representation, with some variations from country to country, albeit knowing its obvious and serious defects. They did it on the grounds of representativeness, with which they are preoccupied to the point of obsession. The cost incurred by this choice is effectiveness and, no doubt, political stability. Nobody will seriously argue that a government formed by one political party instead of several has a better chance of successfully implementing drastic changes. In addition, in such a case responsibility is clear-cut; everybody knows whom to blame or whom to praise, whatever the circumstances. Everybody nowadays is aware that an electoral system based on the "first-past-the-pole" principle (such as that in Britain) usually leads to a single-party government, since through the electoral process the number of parties elected to parliament is reduced drastically (there are rarely more than three). The proportional representation election system generally produces a fragmented parliament.

In the early 1920s there were thirty-four parties in the Sejm (lower house) in Poland and thirteen parties (plus independent deputies) in Czechoslovakia.[52] In the first free Polish elections after communism's collapse, twenty-nine parties were represented in the Sejm. In the 1990–91 elections, Czechoslovakia, Hungary, and Bulgaria each fielded a dozen or more parties. Why the East Europeans, unlike, say, Britain and its former colonies, prefer representativeness to stability and the resultant effective rule is unclear. Certainly not everything can be blamed on tradition and the force of habit; otherwise nothing would ever change, which, as we know, is not the case.[53]

Linked to electoral systems are party systems: Both have an impact on political stability under democracy. Recall that the election system in itself may only inflate or deflate the number of political parties represented in parliament and in this fashion indirectly increase or decrease chances of political stability. In contrast, the party system of moderated competition among nonextremist parties directly results in a stable democracy. How to achieve this highly desirable situation is only vaguely comprehended among the practitioners of politics. A discussion of that topic belongs to the sphere of *political culture*, also an obscure term, and seems to be connected to people's expectations during a period of a revolutionary change. Likely, few will argue with the view that generally speaking people's expectations should be kept low to eschew subsequent disaffection, political apathy, or even worse, disillusionment with democracy and gravitation toward extremist political forces hostile to politics based on free and fair elections.[54]

Yet apart from the Czech Republic, the rest of Eastern Europe, including Russia, initially underwent a revolution of rising expectations triggered by their newly elected leaders. This was an exercise in irresponsible political behavior that several years later resulted in widespread political apathy, distrust of political parties, and lack of voter identity with a party. In the mid-1990s, approximately one in four voters was a committed partisan, which demonstrates vividly how very fickle voter support is for political parties.[55] Several years after 1989 the pure proportional system was somehow modified in several countries—for instance, in Poland—resulting instantly in a drastic reduction of the number of parties represented in parliament (from nearly thirty to five in the 1997 general election). Will this amendment of the electoral system contribute to political stability in that country? Only the future will show. Of course, volatility of the electorate creates negativity, as a rule, an economic transformation thus contributing even further to political instability in many countries.

Some observers of the East European political scene contend that the development of mass political parties in the region is unlikely; rather "formations with loose electorate constituencies, in which a relatively unimportant role is played by the party membership and the dominant role by party leaders" is envisaged.[56] It is telling, however, that not in a single postcommunist state has there been a successful military coup thus far. With the passage of time, though, the likelihood of this happening is on the decline; nonetheless, that it may happen cannot be completely rejected, nor can the establishment of a dictatorship by peaceful means through an electoral process. The communists' loss of power and their subsequent return to it in some countries due to their electoral success several years later should be regarded as a vote for democracy as well; that is, voters prefer, at least at the moment, to change governments and their policies by casting votes, not grenades. The span of time that has elapsed since the fall of communism is, however, too short to indicate how lasting this state of affairs is.

To enhance nascent democracies' chances of survival, political mistrust and cynicism, now so prevalent, ought to be got rid of. Legitimation of the new order and trust of citizens for their political leaders are needed to complete the fundamental change. Political elites must play positive role models. If, for instance, politicians are seen as corrupt, they cannot effectively demand austerity from the voters. Morality in politics plays an important role and can be greatly influenced by law. Where there is no law, corruption, nepotism, and crime are rife. Although without the rule of law democracy may exist, it seems, but only for a while, and even then it is seriously weakened and is rather a mockery of it. The notion of the rule of law means that both rulers and the ruled are bound by it, otherwise it is not law but something else. Though many political leaders despise law for obvious reasons—as a lack of it facilitates, to put it mildly, their exercise of power—people love it because it gives them protection from the powerful state. In a situation where nobody is above the law, that is, when the rule of law prevails, democracy flourishes. This, however, is what Eastern Europe lacks greatly at a time when it needs it most. Not just ordinary people but the business community also wants it, as in uncertain conditions where the rules of the game are unclear business does not prosper nor does the national economy.[57]

What further enhances political stability in a country during a period of fundamental transformation is an adequate policy of economic compensation for groups that are hurt or displaced by economic change, especially the unemployed and people who live on old age pensions as well as large families. Failure to resolve poverty and "safety-net" issues in Russia and Poland has already threatened to derail economic transformation and has jeopardized the process of democratization. A properly executed social security policy can reduce poverty, thus assisting to sustain the painful economic transformation and thereby fostering democracy.[58]

Hitherto arguments and evidence for and against comprehensive change have been examined. The matter has not been settled once and for all. We cannot say who is right and who is wrong in that respect. Yet proponents of both views argue that to secure successful implementation of a democracy and a market economy, relying only on comprehensive or partial fundamental change is not enough. Crucial to the transformation is also the pace or speed of change, which should not be confused with thoroughness, as these two are different phenomena altogether.

The question posed here is at what pace should a fundamental change from one political and economic system to another proceed? As in the above case concerning thoroughness, once again two conflicting views emerged. Some people argue that the best chances of successful transformation are when systemic change is introduced slowly. Their opponents maintain that only through fast change is success increasingly likely.

Supporters of gradual or slow change claim that the go-slow approach is superior to the other because it allows elimination of errors while transformation takes place. In their opinion fast change either does not allow for adjustments to be made or makes adjustments costly. To put it differently, the slow approach has room for flexibility, thereby facilitating the introduction of systemic change with less pain than otherwise possible. One supporter contending along theses lines, stated, "I argue that a gradual approach to privatization—measured in pace and proceeding from the bottom up—is the most appropriate as it allows for greater adaption to change."[59] Why a fast pace of change does not allow for an equal level of adaption he failed to demonstrate, however.

Another advocate of a slow pace of change goes so far as to argue that "really fast restructuring, which is the East German solution, is a policy likely to be socially and politically suicidal in the other post-communist countries,"[60] by which he meant that such a policy would not succeed, but his reasons are unclear. It seems, generally speaking, that all those who countenance a slow pace of change share the view that it will result in social peace, political stability, and only a negligible decline in the standards of living. In that sense, to proceed the other way is likely to be "suicidal" as it may culminate in social unrest, political instability, and a serious decline in the standards of living. In such circumstances, the ultimate outcome of fundamental changes might be unexpected to those who implement them and even opposite to what they have struggled for. They also maintain that the present systemic-wide transformation is unprecedented, and therefore there are no signposts showing which way to go or how fast to proceed. In such a situation, so the argument goes, caution is required, meaning a slow pace is preferable to a fast one.

Adherents of a quick pace claim that it does not mean instant change; change cannot be achieved overnight, but it must be swift to ensure success. Democracy and a market economy will not be attained if the pace of change is slow because, among other things, slow change gives democracy's enemies sufficient time to defend their vested interests. Only when change is swift, however painful it is, are chances of succeeding great as vested interests are destroyed. Furthermore, it is pointed out, peaceful, negotiated systemic change, as is occurring in Eastern Europe now, has less chance of being accomplished than change executed violently, say, through a victory in war. Historical evidence demonstrates that to abolish vested interests is easier and happens more often as a result of war than when peace prevails.

To prolong fundamental change is to extend people's sufferings; therefore, one of the key elements for success in systemic change is the time factor.[61] To reiterate the argument, politicians responsible for transformation have not got plenty of time; they are short not only of capital but of time as well. "The slower the destruction of the old system, the more trouble and pain the transition brings."[62] The fact that economic change generally exacts severe cost immediately but produces benefits only gradually shows that in order to reduce the period of suffering these changes ought to be carried out speedily. People will generally accept a fair amount of hardship for a while, but their patience is limited. It is asserted that "speed [of fundamental change] was of the essence both in breaking the power of the old communist *apparat* and in erecting defenses against the counter attacks [thereafter]."[63]

Although a slow pace of transformation postpones the tangible results of change to a distant future, it generates simultaneously an increasing hostility toward the new order, which has already brought about the unexpected return to power of former communists in a few Eastern European states.[64] It is contended, therefore, that mistakes resulting from swift transformation can be corrected, whereas those stemming from slow change may turn out to be enduring, sometimes even impossible to eradicate and thereby resulting in something other than a liberal democracy and a market economy. "Speed is absolutely essential," declared one of its advocates, "if systemic transformation is not to fizzle out or drop down the black hole of good intentions."[65]

Also, it is pointed out that even though the communist economy can be swiftly dismantled, to create another sustainable market economy takes a long time. The point is, to cut the time short as much as possible is to enhance a market economy's chances of success. The sooner the electorate will benefit economically, the stronger will be its support of the new political order. To prolong the period of change will not result in slowing economic suffering, the argument goes; to the contrary, to delay it makes life more difficult for many people. It has been noted that "economic 'gradualism' is not necessarily coupled with liberal political democracy," but it may end up in new authoritarianism.[66]

Another moot point concerning fundamental transformation is its sequencing, that is, the order in which it ought to occur. People who addressed that question disagree whether fundamental change should proceed step by step, in an ordered sequence, or alternatively, all changes taking place more or less simultaneously. At question is which of these two modes of action gives greater chances for successfully completing the transformation, ending up as it was intended at the beginning, with a prospering market economy and an entrenched liberal democracy.

Proponents of sequencing contend that to secure ultimate success, political change must be separated, in time, from economic change. If the economic transformation from a command to a market economy precedes political transformation from a communist dictatorship to a democracy, the risk involved in the entire operation is greatly reduced compared to a simultaneous change comprising both politics and economics. To introduce political change first and economics second is, in their view, the least likely to succeed, since a combination of a democratic system coupled with a communist economy will simply not work. Why? Because when the electorate does not see tangible material benefits soon, and under the communist economic system this is ruled out, then it will most likely opt for an authoritarian regime. Today, it is claimed, people associate democracy with opulence, believing that this particular political system somehow generates wealth for all. If this does not occur, however, disaffection will follow with disastrous results for democracy. That sequence of change must therefore be avoided. Only the opposite sequence of change will, in all likelihood, bring the desired outcome.

To implement fundamental economic transformation under a dictatorship is easier, so it is asserted, than under a democracy. Even if the people are unhappy with the change, they cannot do much about it, and the rulers know it. To change state policies or governments of dictatorial regimes through popular pressure is difficult, even rare, and when it occurs usually involves bloodshed. Since everybody is aware of this, dictatorial regimes have a degree of political stability and room for economic maneuvers unparalleled in democracy. Because the process of economic transformation requires a relatively long time to complete, impatient voters disappointed with immediate results will cast their votes for the enemies of democracy. In support of their opinion, proponents of this view point to several East Asian countries that successfully transformed their backward economies into prosperous market economies under nondemocratic regimes. The examples of Singapore, South Korea, and Taiwan, countries that yesterday were poor but today are relatively rich with a steadily increasing standard of living, should be imitated by the East European countries because those Asians proved that their way of tackling the economy is working. Also "theories of collective action suggest," according to proponents, "that market reforms must precede democratic consolidation if liberalization is to succeed."[67]

People who support these views perceive democratic regimes as politically weak and unable, because of their weakness, to enforce attempted transformation or to enforce the law that protects citizenship rights, to boot. Under democratic rule politicians are tempted, it is argued, to hold back the market and perpetuate state intervention in the economy, thereby derailing the process of change. Critics have no doubt that

> the current intellectual debate on the "sequencing" of economic and political liberalization suggests that the simultaneous effort to introduce a market economy and democracy will fail in the post-communist world. Weak democracies will impede the project of economic liberalization, because society will not accept the painful effects of price reform, a reduction in welfare benefits [and other costs].[68]

Yet there are others who argue that the creation of a market economy is a necessary but not sufficient condition for the establishment of a democracy; civil society must also exist before democracy strikes roots. As "civil society [cannot exist] without a market," the right order of change is market first, to be followed by civil society; finally, the way is paved for democracy to emerge.[69] With regard to sequencing within the field of economy there is much disagreement, too. Should price liberalization, for instance, precede privatization, or vice versa? Should the domestic economy be protected from international competition until transformation is completed, or should it be exposed to it instantly, a day after communism's collapse? The list of what to do in what order seems endless, and even among those who argue for an ordered sequence of actions there is no consensus about what comes first, what second, and so forth.

Adversaries of sequencing argue on two grounds for simultaneous change comprising all spheres of public life. First, there is no certainty which of the envisaged changes should be introduced at the very onset, and which should follow it, and in what order. Second, they say, we live in a complex world where almost everything is connected with everything else; hence it is extremely difficult, if not impossible, to establish without a doubt the impact one change has on another. Can we measure it? Since we can neither establish the order of priorities with great certainty nor know exactly how any single change will affect the others, it is better to introduce all changes at once, watch what happens, and correct it, if required. There is one more important reason why fundamental transformation ought to be executed in "one go" and that relates to the previously discussed pace. Obviously, simultaneous change in all spheres of public life takes much less time than sequenced change. As mentioned earlier, time matters; the shorter it is, the better, reducing the period of the painful process of transformation experienced by most people and thereby enhancing chances of success.

As one scholar put it: "Ideally, the required changes should follow each other in an ordered sequence of operations. However, since the reform measures are interconnected, it is difficult to introduce one measure without introducing another."[70] Opponents of sequencing add that the need to introduce all changes at once arises from the "holistic" nature of systems, "their essentially integrated order."[71] And as all components of a market economy are interdependent, it does not really matter much which comes first and which follows.

In their view, to introduce political change based on democratic principles at the same time as economic change gives a better chance of success in both areas than to begin with economic transformation alone under an authoritarian regime. The reason is simple: Under a democracy the electorate has an impact on the state and its policies; if dissatisfied with them, it may lawfully change the government or its policies or both. The new political leaders may, and rightly so, blame disastrous economic results on their predecessors and modify the process of economic transformation in a way perceived by them as the most effective. The democratic, peaceful process of economic modifications (and others as well) is endless; it brings, it is argued, social peace, political stability, and perhaps even prosperity as it nourishes the principle of learning by doing—that is, of learning through experience or, as it is sometimes called, by trial an error, the most productive way to succeed.

In addition, it has been observed that the apparent economic success of several East Asian states has not been translated as yet into exemplary democracies. These countries, though now possessing a market economy and wealth, are still authoritarian regimes with unclear prospects for democracy. It follows, so this argument goes, that introduction of a market economy, however successful, does not necessarily bring about democracy. Thus, if one desires both a market economy and democracy, the two must be introduced roughly at the same time, each for its own sake.

The sheer impossibility of finding a clear-cut solution to the intractable issue of sequencing may have prompted the future prime minister of the Czech Republic, Vaclav Klaus, to argue for "the introduction of as many changes as possible, as quickly as possible" without worrying unduly about the order in which they occur.[72]

One highly desirable outcome of this approach is the destruction of vested interests, and in that sense it is similar to a comprehensive approach to fundamental transformation, each of them reinforcing the other and thus paving the way to liberal democracy and a market economy better than under any other scenario. For that reason, among others, those who contend that the changes must occur in "one go" also advocate a comprehensive transformation. The question remains whether the East European governments have the capacity to "deliver the goods," to bring about wealth and sustainable democracy. James Madison in one of *The Federalist Papers* written over 200 years ago contended that "a good government implies two things; first, fidelity to the object of government, which is the happiness of the people; secondly, a knowledge of the means by which that object can be best obtained."[73] In his opinion, "some governments are deficient in both these qualities: most governments are deficient in the first."[74] "The true test of a good government," concluded Alexander Hamilton, "is its aptitude and tendency to produce a good administration."[75]

Yet for a successful transformation from communism to democracy and a market economy to be completed to adopt proper scope, pace, and sequencing is, it seems to some, not enough. The former communist regimes of Eastern Europe are perceived by nearly everybody as unjust. Admittedly, most people hoped that the collapse of communism would bring a new political order based on justice. However difficult it is to define justice, in specific circumstances we know its meaning and can easily recognize it. Perhaps that was the reason that prompted Gottfried Wilhelm Leibniz to write in that respect that "it is true that you do not see justice as you see a horse, but you understand it no less, or rather you understand it better."[76]

Under communist rule many individuals blamed injustice on the lack of democracy and assumed that when democracy superseded communism justice would prevail.[77] "Justice is the end of government. It is the end of civil society," declared James Hamilton.[78] Yet others maintain that justice is instrumental as well; it is a means to an end. For national economy to grow and for people to prosper, government rule must be firmly entrenched on the principle of justice. Adam Smith in his famous *Wealth of Nations* argued along these lines when he wrote:

> Commerce and manufacturers can seldom flourish long in any state which does not enjoy a regular administration of justice, in which the people do not feel themselves secure in the possession of their property, in which the faith of contracts is not supported by law. . . . Commerce and manufacturers, in short, can seldom flourish in any state in which there is not a certain degree of confidence in the justice of government.[79]

One glance over Eastern Europe now, however, is sufficient to come to the conclusion that whatever fundamental transformation occurred on there since the fall of communism, injustice remains widespread and justice is in short supply. This gives gloomy prospects for democracy and economic prosperity in postcommunist societies. Of course, the situation in that regard varies from country to country, generally deteriorating as one proceeds from the West to the East. It is better, for instance, in the Czech Republic than in Russia, and better in former East Germany than, say, in Poland. As a former East German political dissident put it: "We struggled for justice; instead we received the rule of law." In other countries of the region, however, there is either very little or no justice or rule of law.[80] This, in turn, brings about frustration, political apathy, and disillusionment with democracy itself.

As mentioned previously, some politicians in Eastern Europe assert that in the present situation, immediately after the demise of communism, to rule on the principle of justice might easily be transformed into a mockery leading to witch-hunts of former communists, resulting in even more injustice. The corollary is that justice should be delayed to an unspecified future; in the meantime mercy should replace it.[81] The fact that in many countries in Eastern Europe today's rulers were communists not long ago, as in Russia, poses an enormous difficulty for justice to prevail. A lack of justice, however, has prompted many persons to claim that little has really changed in their countries since the collapse of communism because one group of unjust rulers has superseded another, and this has not benefited ordinary people.[82] It is often pointed out that those who committed crimes under communist rule are rarely punished for them now. Furthermore, a number of former party *apparatchiks* are today the richest people in their countries; they are always successful. Frequently they secured their newly acquired wealth illegally. Is that justice, ask ordinary people?

By the late 1990s transformation from a communist economy to one based on private property and market forces has been completed in one country only, namely, former East Germany, which in October 1990 was unified with West Germany. This makes it a unique operation, but nonetheless it would be useful to examine it, however briefly, assuming that an important lesson can be learned from it.

Unlike all other East European states, the Germans decided to execute the transformation of the East German economy not through the government but through a separate agency established for that purpose, called Treuhandanstalt. The presumption was that if something went wrong, the agency would be blamed, not the government. In addition, it was thought, a separate body instituted to implement that task would be immune, or almost immune, from political pressure, thereby increasing chances of success.

The results achieved hitherto are impressive, making former East Germany the fastest growing region in Europe. Since 1992 its economy has grown between 7 and 10 percent per year.[83] "Purely in terms of living standards, East Germans are the clear winners of communism's collapse."[84] Within three years of being established, the Treuhand Agency sold 95 percent of former East Germany's state-owned enterprises.[85]

According to a Treuhand official, the lessons of this agency's privatization for Eastern Europe are the necessity for speed and the value of a privatization agency independent of government. In his opinion, three factors make rapid privatization a positive element of economic transformation. First, privatization brings about eventual "economic rationalization." Because newly established private enterprises as a rule do not receive government support, either they will make a profit or go bankrupt. Second, rapid privatization immediately removes the financial burden from the government, thus saving taxpayers' money for other purposes. Finally, as observed, privatization becomes more difficult to achieve as time passes; hence it should be done at an early stage, soon after the collapse of communism.[86]

Such rapid economic transformation, compared to the rest of Eastern Europe, could hardly have been achieved only on the amount of capital available, though that amount was huge. Certainly, the Germans possessed much more capital than anybody else in the region, and they used their money to transform state property into private property. In addition to that, however, they had the know-how—the expertise with and the firsthand experience of modern markets. As much as capital, these factors belonging to the sphere of business culture played a crucial role during the transformation. And these are exactly what the rest of Eastern Europe lacks. What this means is that in other countries the goal of obtaining a successful economic transformation will be much more difficult to realize than it was for East Germany, and perhaps it will not be achieved in the foreseeable future by all.

The following chapter discusses in detail the move from communism to capitalism and democracy in Russia.

NOTES

1. Edmund Burke, *Reflections on the Revolution in France* (Boston: Little Brown, 1901), p. 102.

2. Perhaps because of this fact the Party of Democratic Socialism (PDS), the successor to the East German communist party, consistently received almost 20 percent of the East German vote at the local state and federal elections in 1994 and nearly 35 percent of the vote in former East Berlin. Jeffrey Kepstein, "Weak Foundations under East German Reconstruction," *Transition*, Vol. 2, 26 January 1996, p. 36.

3. Ibid.

4. These countries are Lithuania, Poland, Hungary, and Bulgaria.

5. Vojtěch Cepl and Mark Gillis, "Making Amends after Communism," *Journal of Democracy*, Vol. 7, No. 4, October 1996, p. 119.

6. "Disappointment and bitterness are growing throughout Eastern Europe as hopes fade for a quick transition to a market economy. The problems East Europeans now face are far more difficult than anything they could imagine two years ago," argues Leif Rosenberger in "Economic Transition in Eastern Europe: Paying the Price for Freedom," *East European Quarterly*, Vol. 27, No. 3, September 1992, p. 261.

7. "Some people argue," wrote Sunley, "that with regard to Eastern Europe acquaintanceship with the past will serve you much better than a knowledge of recent events. Indeed, in this part of the world, to know the past—especially the distant past—*is* [emphasis in the original] to understand the present." Johnathan Sunley, "Post-Communism: An Infantile Disorder," *The National Interest*, No. 4, summer 1996, p. 3.

8. Ibid.

9. Alexis de Tocqueville, *Democracy in America* (New York: New American Library, 1956), p. 39.

10. Andrew Janos, "Continuity and Change in Eastern Europe: Strategies of Post-Communist Politics," in Beverley Crawford (ed.), *Markets, States and Democracy: The Political Economy of Post-Communist Transformation* (Boulder, CO: Westview Press, 1995), p. 153. According to Ivan T. Berend, "there was a rather limited pre-history of self-financing, self-regulating market capitalism and liberal market ideology in Eastern Europe. Lateness, backwardness, and peripheral status were not only economic issues but generated special social structures, political reactions, movements, and ideologies as well. The automatism of a well-functioning market economy hardly ever worked in these peripheral societies." Ivan T. Berend, "Alternatives of Transformation: Choices and Determinants—East-Central Europe in the 1990s," in Crawford (ed.), pp. 138–139.

11. Alice H. Amsden, Jacek Kochanowicz, and Lance Taylor, *The Market Meets Its Match: Restructuring the Economies of Eastern Europe* (Cambridge, MA: Harvard University Press, 1994), p. 159.

12. Stephen Fischer-Galati, "The Political Right in Eastern Europe in Historical Perspective," in Joseph Held (ed.), *Democracy and Right-Wing Politics in Eastern Europe in the 1990's* (Boulder, CO: East European Monographs, 1993), p. 11.

13. Dezso Kovacs and Sally Ward Maggard, "The Human Face of Political, Economic, and Social Change in Eastern Europe," *East European Quarterly*, Vol. 27, No. 3, September 1993, p. 340.

14. Jan S. Prybyla, "The Road from Socialism: Why, Where, What and How?" *Problems of Communism*, Vol. 40, Nos. 1–2, January-April 1991, pp. 9–10.

15. Henryk Flakierski, "Market Socialism Revisited: An Alternative for Eastern Europe," *International Journal of Sociology*, Vol. 25, No. 3, fall 1995, p. 95.

16. Barbara Kling, "Blood, Sweat, or Cheating: Politics and the Transformation of Socialist Economies in China, the USSR, and Eastern Europe," *Studies in Comparative Communism*, Vol. 24, No. 2, June 1991, p. 148.

17. *The Australian*, 7 March 1997.

18. Daniel S. Fogel and Suzanne Etcheverry, "Performing the Economics of Central and Eastern Europe," in Daniel S. Fogel (ed.), *Managing in Emerging Market Economies* (Boulder, CO: Westview Press, 1994), p. 33.

19. Zhelyu Zhelev, "Is Communism Returning?" *Journal of Democracy*, Vol. 7, No. 3, July 1996, p. 5.

20. Beverly Crawford, "Post-Communist Political Economy: A Framework for the Analysis of Reform" in Crawford (ed.), ibid., p. 16.

21. Anders Åslund, "The Case for Radical Reform," *Journal of Democracy*, Vol. 5, No. 4, October 1994, p. 69.

22. Datuk Seri Mahathir bin Mohamad, quoted by Jose Maria Maravall, "The Myth of the Authoritarian Advantage," *Journal of Democracy*, Vol. 5, No. 4, October 1994, pp. 17–18.

23. Ibid.

24. Åslund, p. 69.

25. Yali Peng, "Privatization in Eastern Europe Countries," *East Europe Quarterly*, Vol. 26, No. 4, January 1993, p. 482.

26. "Rozmowa z Miltonem i Rose Friedmanami," *Wprost*, No. 32, August 1996, p. 18.

27. Åslund, p. 73.

28. Bernard Chavance, *The Transformation of Communist Systems: Economic Reforms since the 1950s* (Boulder, CO: Westview Press, 1994), p. 212.

29. Adam Przeworski, *Democracy and the Market: Political and Economic Reforms in Eastern Europe and Latin America* (Cambridge: Cambridge University Press, 1991), p. 190.

30. Bill Lomax, "Impediments to Democratization in Post-Communist East-Central Europe," in Gordon Wightman (ed.), *Party Formation in East-Central Europe* (Aldershot, England: Edward Elgar, 1995), p. 179.

31. "Rozmowa z Miltonem i Rose Friedmanami," p. 18. See also Robert A. Dahl, "Why Free Markets Are Not Enough," *Journal of Democracy*, Vol. 3, No. 3, July 1992, pp. 86–87.

32. László Csaba, for instance, argues that mere "ownership change may lead to private monopolies with no efficiency gains." See László Csaba "The Political Economy of the Reform Strategy: China and Eastern Europe Compared," *Communist Economies and Economic Transformation*, Vol. 8, No. 1, March 1996, p. 61.

33. Hans Keman, however, argues to the contrary. In his opinion, "the model of 'mixed economy' is not only appropriate, but also it contributes to a better understanding of the present problems of democratization." See Hans Keman, "Managing the Mixed Economy in Central and Eastern Europe: Democratic Politics and the Role of the Public Sector," *Democratization*, Vol. 3, No. 2, summer 1996, p. 111.

34. Susan C. Stokes, "Public Opinion and Market Reforms: The Limits of Economic Voting," *Comparative Political Studies*, Vol. 29, No. 5, October 1996, p. 502.

35. Ibid., p. 516. See also Francis Fukuyama, "Capitalism and Democracy: The Missing Link," *Journal of Democracy*, Vol. 3, No. 3, July 1992, pp. 100–110.

36. Giovanni Sartori, "How Far Can Free Government Travel," *Journal of Democracy*, Vol. 6, No. 3, July 1995, p. 106. According to Friedrich Levcik, "Transition from stabilization to growth is politically imperative [because] people are losing the enthusiasm and willingness for sacrifice which they felt immediately" after the fall of communism. See Friedrich Levcik, "Economic Transformation in the East: A Critical Appraisal of Its Development and Suggestions for a Possible Way Out," in Christopher T. Saunders (ed.), *Eastern Europe in Crisis and the Way Out* (London: Macmillan, 1995), p. 26.

37. Vilfredo Pareto, *The Transformation of Democracy* (edited with an introduction by Charles H. Powers) (New Brunswick, NJ: Transaction Books, 1984), p. 63.

38. Francis Fukuyama, "'The Primacy of Culture," *Journal of Democracy*, Vol. 6, No. 1, January 1995, p. 14.

39. Samuel P. Huntington, "Democracy's Third Wave," *Journal of Democracy*, Vol. 2, No. 2, spring 1991, pp. 22–23.

40. Aviezer Tucker, "Wrestling the Entrenched Education Bureaucracy," *Transition*, Vol. 2, No. 12, 14 January 1996, p. 47.

41. Jerzy Hausner, Bob Jessop, and Klaus Nielsen (eds.), *Strategic Choice and Path-Dependency in Post-Socialism* (Aldershot, England: Edward Elgar, 1995), p. 6.

42. Michael Radu, "Western Diasporas in Post-Communist Transitions," *Problems of Post-Communism*, Vol. 42, No. 3, May-June 1995, pp. 60–61.

43. *The Times*, 24 September 1996; and *The New York Times*, 16 November 1996. For instance, the leader of Croatia, President Franjo Tudjman, underwent cancer treatment at a Washington hospital. Also, when the Russian president, Boris Yeltsin, had a heart problem in 1996, U.S. doctor Michael DeBakey went to Moscow for consultations about whether to operate on the gravely ill Yeltsin.

44. See, for example, Peter Tamasi, "The Role of Social Sciences in the Central and East European Transformation Process," *International Social Science Journal*, No. 148, June 1996, pp. 272–273. See also Teresa Torańska, *My* (Warsaw: Oficyna Wydawnicza MOST, 1994), p. 178.

45. David Hume, *An Inquiry Concerning Human Understanding* (Indianapolis: Liberal Arts Press, 1995), p. 43.

46. Michael G. Roskin, "The Emerging Party Systems of Central and Eastern Europe," *East European Quarterly*, Vol. 27, No. 1, March 1993, p. 60.

47. Quoted by Jane Perlez, "For Hungarian Army Officers, It's 'Eyes West!,' " *The New York Times*, January 2, 1997.

48. Piotr Sztompka, "Looking Back: The Year 1989 as a Cultural and Civilizational Break," *Communist and Post-Communist Studies*, Vol. 29, No. 2, June 1996, p. 126.

49. Robert A. Dahl, "The Problem of Civic Competence," *Journal of Democracy*, Vol. 3, No. 4, October 1992, p. 45.

50. Max Weber, *The Protestant Ethics and the Spirit of Capitalism* (London: Routledge, 1930), pp. 35–78 passim.

51. Ralph Dahrendorf, *Reflections on the Revolution in Europe* (New York: Times Books, Random House, 1990), p. 106. See also Teresa Torańska, ibid., pp. 57–59.

52. Roskin, p. 60.

53. Stanisław Gomułka's wholehearted support for a proportional representation system is typical for people who do not perceive effective government and political stability as crucial to the nascent democracies' survival. According to him, after the collapse of communism, "none of the parties has a record and they are therefore unknown quantities to the electorate. The large pool is therefore an asset in the sense that it enhances political competition, promotes tolerance and offers small parties the chance of becoming winners. Perhaps more importantly, it also reduces the risk of political alienation by large sections of the electorate, the risk of groups under represented in parliaments seeking to influence the political

process through extra-parliamentary means. The political reformers face here a trade off between instability of governments and instability of countries." In Stanisław Gomułka, "Economic and Political Constraints during Transition," *Europe-Asia Studies*, Vol. 46, No. 1, 1994, p. 104.

54. Roskin, p. 47.

55. Richard Rose, "Mobilizing Demobilized Voters in Post-Communist Societies," *Party Politics*, Vol. 1, No. 4, 1995, p. 549.

56. Peter Kopecki, "Developing Party Organizations in East-Central Europe," *Party Politics*, Vol. 1, No. 4, 1995, p. 517.

57. It is the state's task to "introduce laws and ensure they are enforced, pursue a fiscal and monetary policy, and exert supervision where this is essential," contends Janos Kornai. See his "Transformation Recession: The Example of Hungary," in Christopher T. Saunders (ed.), *Eastern Europe in Crisis and the Way Out* (London: Macmillan, 1995), p. 62.

58. Carol Grahm, "The Politics of Safety Nets," *Journal of Democracy*, Vol. 6, No. 2, April 1995, pp. 152–154.

59. Kazimierz Z. Poznański, "Political Economy of Privatization in Eastern Europe," in Beverley Crawford (ed.), p. 204.

60. Stanisław Gomułka, "Polish Economic Reform, 1990–1991: Principles, Policies and Outcomes," *Cambridge Journal of Economics*, No. 16, 1992, p. 370.

61. Louis Haddad, "On the Rational Sequencing of Enterprise Reform," *Journal of Communist Studies and Transitional Politics*, Vol. 11, No. 1, March 1995, p. 93.

62. Åslund, p. 64.

63. Ibid.

64. Ivan Major, "The Decay of the Command Economics," *Eastern European Politics and Societies*, Vol. 8, No. 2, spring 1994, p. 343.

65. Prybyla, p. 9.

66. Crawford (ed.), p. 31.

67. Ibid., p. 4.

68. Ibid.

69. Giuseppe Di Palma, "Why Democracy Can Work in Eastern Europe," *Journal of Democracy*, Vol. 2, No. 1, winter 1991, p. 28.

70. Haddad, p. 92.

71. Prybyla, p. 10.

72. Quoted by Haddad, p. 92.

73. Gary Will (ed.), *The Federalist Papers by Alexander Hamilton, James Madison and John Jay* (New York: Bantam Books 1982; first published in 1787–88). Federalist paper No. 62, p. 316.

74. Ibid.

75. Ibid., p. 346.

76. Patrick Riley (ed.), *Leibniz: Political Writings* (Cambridge: Cambridge University Press, 1972), p. 205.

77. Ian Shapiro, "Elements of Democratic Justice," *Political Theory*, Vol. 24, No. 4, November 1996, p. 579.

78. In Will (ed.), p. 265. His view is shared by Ralph Dahrendorf, *Reflections on the Revolution in Europe* (New York: Times Book, Random House, 1990), p. 102.

79. Quoted in Stanley Kober, "The French Revolution, the American Revolution, and Russia Today," *Problems of Post-Communism*, Vol. 42, No. 5, September-October 1995, p. 52.

80. Torańska, p. 108.

81. That is the view of the well-known former Polish dissident Adam Michnik.

82. Torańska, 109.

83. Jeffrey Kopstein, "Weak Foundations under East German Reconstruction," *Transition*, Vol. 2, No. 2, 26 January 1996, p. 34.

84. Ibid., p. 64.

85. Jorg Roesler, "Privatization in Eastern Germany—Experience with the Treuhand," *Europe-Asia Studies*, Vol. 46, No. 3, 1994, p. 565.

86. Emil Nagengast, "Eastern Europe and Germany's Treuhandanstalt," *East European Quarterly*, Vol. 29, No. 2, June 1995, p. 200.

3 Russia: Carpetbaggers' Country

Never in its political history has Russia gone through such a fundamental, revolutionary transformation as it is undergoing now. All previous attempts at change—those initiated by Ivan the Terrible, Peter the Great, and the Bolsheviks—were political reforms that strengthened the authoritarian regime, whereas the changes introduced by the Soviet leader Mikhail Gorbachev resulted, rather unexpectedly to its author, in a fundamental systemic transformation unprecedented in Russia's 1,000-year existence. With an impact reaching far beyond Russia's borders, this phenomenon is only vaguely appreciated in both the West and in Russia itself.

Since Gorbachev came to power in 1985, Eastern European states have regained independence; the Soviet Union has disintegrated; Czechoslovakia, East Germany, and Yugoslavia have ceased to exist, and communism collapsed in virtually all Soviet-dominated states and former Soviet republics. The Moscow-led military alliance, the Warsaw Pact, no longer exists; neither does the Soviet controlled East European economic organization COMECON.

After Gorbachev's resignation in December 1991, his successor, Boris Yeltsin, in effect embarked upon systemic transformation aimed at changing Russia into a democratic state with a national economy based on market forces. Because Russia had never before experienced democracy and knew very little, if anything, of the market economy, Yeltsin's dual mission began nothing less than a revolution, perhaps the first revolution in Russia really deserving the name.

The fifteen Soviet republics converted into independent states, of which the Russian Federation is the largest in terms of its size and population. It comprises approximately 150 million people and 17 million square kilometers thus remains the largest state in the world. Although economically and politically seriously weakened in recent years, it is nuclear power to be reckoned with.

Under the rule of Boris Yeltsin, Russia went through several parliamentary elections and a presidential election as well. At the same time a large part of the national economy was privatized and to a certain degree exposed to the operations of a free market. The ongoing systemic change in the sphere of economics, namely, a move from a command to a market economy is, it seems, no less important for Russia than its political change from authoritarianism to democracy.

The revolutionary change Russia is now undergoing has affected virtually everybody, causing much misery as well as many disappointments. There are a few winners as well, that is, people who have become fabulously rich almost overnight. Yet many people live in poverty even by Russian standards, sometimes under conditions worse than those endured under the old communist regime. Russians disappointed with the nascent democracy and growing market economy, both completely alien to them, are in increasing numbers shifting their support from parties that opt for democracy to those that are against it. Accompanying the systemic change are a growing crime rate, unemployment (previously unknown), lack of rule of law, corruption, and inflation, which in turn generate political apathy, feelings of insecurity, and loss of hope for a better future.

That Russia never experienced democracy before does not by itself mean that the country's current efforts to achieve it are doomed to failure. What that means, simply, is that it will not be easy to attain an enduring stable democracy without achieving at the same time a meaningful economic success, that is, one that will result in a higher standard of living for the majority of Russians. Because many people today associate wealth with democracy, the fate of democracy in Russia is closely linked to the country's economic progress.

In that context the question to be asked is whether the Russian political leadership is willing and able to deliver the economic "goodies." Russia's political future depends on the answer to this question. Paradoxically, the results achieved by the Russians since the collapse of communism are impressive and unimpressive. They are not impressive in comparison to those attained, say, by the Czechs. They are, however, very impressive in comparison to those of previous Russian tsarist and communist attempts to change the country politically and economically. Whereas the Czechs are restoring what they lost due to unhappy circumstances, the Russians are aiming for what they never had before, namely, democracy and a market economy. That the Russians have attained a democracy, however fragile, and an economy that is not a communist one, albeit hardly a market economy, means that they have come a longer way than have the Czechs, relatively speaking. Certainly, to walk a familiar path is easier than to travel the unknown road, and it offers the traveler a greater chance to achieve his destiny than otherwise.

The ultimate outcome of the ongoing Russian revolution is not a foregone conclusion, however; many things may happen in the foreseeable future to affect strongly the nascent Russian democracy. Because democracy and the free market are not well entrenched in Russia as a result of Russia's lack of experience of them and the short passage of time since the change began, it is extremely difficult to predict the end result of the current transformation. Yet this is not to contend that Russia's authoritarian political tradition and its collectivist approach to economy is going to prevail. Moscow's current politics and economy is in a volatile state, and this may continue for some time. It is the argument of this chapter that the ultimate outcome of the systemic transformation in Russia is uncertain.

The transition from reform to revolution distinguishes the Gorbachev and Yeltsin era from all former reform attempts in Russia and the Soviet Union and indicates a successful departure from the apparent cycle of unfinished transformation.[1] Consensus prevails that in its systemic change, especially in the sphere of its economy, Russia lags behind several East European states, including the Czech Republic. Decollectivization of agriculture has made little progress since the collapse of communism toward the end of 1991.[2] Although a large part of Russia's national economy outside agriculture has been privatized, the results borne are unimpressive. Many Russians are experiencing a steadily deteriorating standard of living, corruption and crime are rife, unemployment is rising, and inflation is high. In the early 1990s two attempts by hard-line communists and nationalists to stop the transformation ended up in unsuccessful bloody coups. The struggle between supporters of fundamental change and its opponents is not yet over.

That split is clearly visible among the Russian political elite.[3] The State Duma, the lower house in the Russian parliament, is dominated by politicians hostile to democracy and the free market, whereas the president and those around him, however hesitantly, support it. Also, the Russian electorate is deeply divided over whether to continue the process of systemic change aimed at achieving Western democracy and a market economy or to return to status quo ante. Six years after Gorbachev resigned and communism collapsed in the Soviet Union half of Russia's population perceives its life as "unbearable."[4] That does not mean, of course, that for the majority of people life under the old regime was bearable or happy. Political change aside, it does mean that the quality of life, in particular the standard of living, has deteriorated significantly for many, with only a few people profiting from the new situation. As one observer has commented, "Unpaid wages and law and order are now the major issues for ordinary people."[5]

Furthermore, it appears that the transformation has not brought with it justice; it rewards "criminals at the expense of ordinary people," thereby making the plight of those who have not succeeded even worse.[6] Who will those disillusioned people support in the next general elections? Why can Russians not keep pace with, say, Hungarians, Poles, or Czechs, or even surpass them in their efforts to effect economic transformation? The Russians lived longer than anybody else under communist rule, and that means that they also suffered longer than other people. Did they not learn more because of this, and do they not know better now how to obtain a prosperous life for all and ensure just rule? The answer is no. The opposite holds true.

Having lived for three generations under communism, where private property was abolished, competition was nonexistent, and the rule of law unknown, Russians will cope less easily with the transformation than those nations who experienced a competive environment in a free market economy before the imposition of communism. What lessens the chances for successful economic change is Russia's lack of experience. Before the 1917 Bolsheviks seizure of power, tsarist Russia also lacked to a large degree a market economy and a judiciary system based on the concept of the rule of law.[7] In other words, the transition from the tsarist authoritarianism to communism was not as great as the Bolsheviks maintained. Some scholars today contend that even after the collapse of communism in Russia there remains "a strong degree of cultural continuity" going back not only to the Soviet era but to tsarist times as well.[8]

Indeed, even a glance at Russia's past shows how little the country changed from the time Ivan the Terrible wielded power to the year Mikhail Gorbachev ascended to the leadership of the Soviet Union. Throughout those periods the Russian regime was authoritarian, and for the most part private property did not exist.[9] Only under the rule of Catherine the Great, in the second half of the eighteenth century, was state ownership of land abolished and private property introduced. Until her rule, the state imposed service obligation on all landholders, in exchange for service to the state, they were assigned land for lifetime use. When the holders died, their land, along with the peasants bound to it, reverted to the state. Abolition of serfdom in Russia, just over a century ago, in 1861, made the peasants free under the law but not in reality. The state remained the ultimate source of almost all material benefits until the communists took over. Once the communists seized power in 1917, private property was abolished once more and with that the state again became the source of material benefits— this time the only source.

This means that the only type of economy known to Russians since the Middle Ages was a command economy. From this it follows that Russia never developed a strong and independent bourgeoisie. The peasants did not break out of patriarchal bondage until 1917, and even afterward, their status was more that of a serf than that of a free citizen.[10] State and collective farms during the Soviet era might be seen as an extension of the old Russian village community, where privately owned land was unknown. Hence, some observers argue, collectivization of agriculture in the Soviet Union may be viewed as a "second enserfment."[11] Perhaps this explains Russians' hostility to private property, so often noticed today by Western observers.[12] An aversion to private property is especially widespread among peasants, who have thus far successfully resisted privatizing state farms. Peasant resistance to private ownership of land is usually attributed to the persistence of a "collectivist popular mentality."[13]

As a result of the authoritarian past Russia had no parliamentary forum for political debate, decision making, and passing of new laws. Political power was concentrated entirely in the hands of one person, the ruler or autocrat. That absolutist tradition survived under Soviet rule in the guise of communist party rule, wherein after Stalin's death a single leader was replaced by an oligarchy. Not until the early twentieth century was an ersatz parliament, called the State Duma, created in Russia. In reality, however, the first four State Dumas, sitting between 1906 and 1916, were nothing more than legislative advisory bodies to the tsar—not a real parliament. The tsar changed the electoral rules at his pleasure and banished recalcitrant deputies to Siberia. Each of the first four Dumas was dissolved by the tsar. After the abolition of the monarchy in 1917, a Constituent Assembly was elected by universal suffrage. The Bolsheviks, who received a minority vote (about one-quarter of ballots cast), forcibly dissolved this first democratically elected parliament in Russian history after one day. Not until the early

1990s did free parliamentary elections take place in Russia again.[14] The first Russian ruler under the name of president was elected in free general election only in 1996, and the first constitution adopted by referendum took place as late as December 1993.[15]

Albeit the new constitution defines the Russian state as a "federation" it is a federation more in name than reality. Can such a large and diverse state be democratic in the long run? Some critics think this unlikely. In their view, "A democratic Russia can survive only as a truly federal state with a much weakened center and strong localities."[16] A united Russian state, according to them, is possible only under an authoritarian regime. To eschew this the critics argue, Russia's regions ought to be made "constituent parts" of the national government.[17] Whether the traditional Russian centralized rule is now coming to an end remains to be seen.

The Russian constitution of 1993 grants the president extensive powers in naming governments, introducing legislation, and making policy. The president can also veto legislation and dissolve parliament. The Russians failed to introduce to the constitution a system of checks and balances that will work, for the separation of powers principle hardly exists in it or, more importantly, in practice.[18] The constitution does not turn Russia into a parliamentary republic nor make it completely a presidential one.[19] The parliament is weak; government is subordinated to the president and does not have to represent the majority party or the coalition party in the Duma or lower house.

Critics also point out that the political party system in Russia is undeveloped. Its experience with the party system is relatively short, starting in the early twentieth century and abruptly ending soon after at the end of World War I. In the wake of the demise of communism in Russia have come a huge number of political parties, but they differ significantly from the parties in the West. In today's Russia politics is highly personalized, and divisions among parties relate less to deficient ideologies and more to personalities. Often political leaders use their parties as instruments in their struggle for personal power.[20] As a result of the weakness of the multiparty system, real power in Russia is concentrated outside the parties, in interest groups, including the army, security forces, business leaders, and the president and those around him, in particular.

The reasons for the weakness of the political party system stem from Russia's past. It is frequently said that for democracy to emerge and last long, prior existence of a civil society is a necessary condition. Civil society denotes an intermediary entity standing between the private domain and the state. It is the sphere of voluntary, organized social life, one that Russia has hardly experienced in its history. Through activity in a variety of voluntary organizations, citizens learn to act responsibly, become accountable for what they do, and obtain organizational and leadership skills. In a nutshell, civil society is a kind of political school for ordinary citizens and their future politicians. Furthermore, the existence of a widespread and dynamic civil society makes the state less ubiquitous, less powerful, thereby increasing the chances of attaining a sustainable democracy. An argument can be made that the stronger the civil society, the stronger the democracy.

In Russia civil society is obviously weak, very weak. The conditions that facilitated the emergence of civil society in the West several centuries ago were missing in Russia until the spectacular fall of the Soviet empire. Admittedly, private ownership helps to establish civil society by making many people become less dependent on the state and, therefore, less afraid of engaging in social activity outside state control. A great incentive for civil society to flourish is the existence of the rule of law because it protects ordinary people against the power of the state. Without law, one can contend, civil society is hardly conceivable. Until recently private property in Russia existed only for a short period, approximately over a century, and the rule of law had a very short life too (from the 1860s to 1881, when a trial by jury ruled). Indeed, the concept of law as a rule binding both the rulers and the ruled is at least as alien to the Russians as the concept of private property. Additional impediments to the emergence of civil society in the country have been the existence of political police since the times of Ivan the Terrible and also of political censorship, which goes back several centuries too.[21]

Unlike elsewhere, a close association between Church and state existed throughout Russian history, with the Church almost completely subjugated to the state during the communist period. Whereas after the imposition of communism in Poland the Church there became a champion of people's rights and was for many years the only enclave independent of state control, such was not the case in Russia, where the Church nearly always remained allied to the state establishment. Whether the Church will now distance itself from the state to become a part of civil society remains to be seen. If this happens, it will give an enormous boost to the emerging civil society and its role in the country's public life.[22]

The postcommunist order in Russia is based upon a limited and qualified commitment to democratic values. Yet it is usually claimed that democratic rule is unlikely to survive unless sustained by a substantial consensus on liberal and democratic values. To achieve a sustainable democracy an agreement among political elites on new "rules of the game" is required. It was through them, to a large extent, that democracy was successfully introduced to Japan and Germany in the wake of World War II.

Furthermore, it is vitally important that a powerful and outspoken middle class be created rapidly because it is this group that is especially interested in establishing the rule of law, free media, and a market economy. The middle class has a vested interest in democracy's survival and further consolidation, since members of this class will profit from the new order and will thus defend it against its enemies. An emergence of a middle class coupled with a market economy usually leads to dispersion of power throughout society, thereby enhancing the new democracy. An accountable government further strengthens a democratic regime; whereas a political system devoid of it is weak and fragile, and it performs poorly. Present-day Russia is an example of the latter, that is, of a poorly performing and politically weak and fragile regime. Accountability usually brings about efficiency, which in turn makes the new regime attractive to ordinary people, who have a stake in its success because they gain materially under the changed circumstances. To ask whether the postcommunist governments of Russia hitherto have been accountable ones is rather a rhetorical question.[23]

Without trust, it is difficult to establish a family, friendship, or the body politic. And trust must be earned. Even a superficial look at the current Russian political scene leads one quickly to conclude that trust is missing from its public life. Indeed, political parties are in the forefront of the organizations that Russians distrust most: Only 7 percent of people have confidence in them.[24] Approximately a sixth of the Russian population generally trusts in representative institutions. Interestingly, institutions that attract trust and inspire people's confidence are those that enforce order— the police, the army, the criminal courts, and the political police (former KGB).[25] That a similar degree of distrust of political organizations and civil institutions has been observed in most East European states is small consolation for Russia. That lack of trust in representative institutions tells much about people's feelings and perceptions of the new order. Also, it is argued, the persistence of distrust in Russia has "stunted the growth of democracy" there.[26]

Naturally there are well-founded reasons for the widespread distrust, and the two most important ones are incompetence and corruption; unsurprisingly, they frequently go together. Incompetent individuals appear more susceptible to corruption than others, especially when conditions encourage larceny, bribery, and nepotism. The state of lawlessness Russia is currently experiencing has made the country a breeding ground for corruption. The very people today entrusted with Russia's economic transformation were in most cases yesterday's communist politicians and economists turned overnight into liberal democrats and free marketeers. However genuine their change of views and however hard their effort, they cannot become instantly efficient and productive in what they do nowadays.[27] What matters here is experience of a market economy and democratic institutions—experience that they do not possess and of which they are usually unaware. They also know that they will not be long in power if they do not deliver the goods they promised because of their incompetence. Given that situation, they try to enrich themselves as quickly as possible, which means abusing the system and its laws; this is the way taken by many and resisted by few.

It is, in addition, contended that "few industrialists or political leaders [in Russia] who advocate postponing democratization have articulated a plan for economic development that reaches beyond enriching themselves with public funds."[28] A serious obstacle to a succesful economic transformation in the country is its people's understanding of market operations. The idea of a transaction mutually beneficial is almost totally alien to Russians, to whom two-person exchange is a zero-sum game in which what one person gains the other loses.[29] The market, to their understanding, is a battleground with winners and losers, with the implication that only certain people, indeed, a small minority, will benefit from an economy based on market principles whereas the overwhelming majority will make up the losers, as in a war.

That view of profit-making in the sphere of the economy is also encountered in political life. To win in politics means to get all one wants, which leaves the other person, by definition, empty-handed. Compromise, that is, a settlement of a dispute by which each side gives up something it has asked for and neither side gets all it has asked for, is "tantamount to treason" for many Russians.[30] In a successful body politic, however, and in liberal democracy in particular, compromise lies at the heart of government; without it liberal democracy is unattainable.

In a 1995 survey of Russian businesspeople approximately one in four admitted making regular payments to criminal organizations, which controlled more than 40,000 businesses, including 550 banks. In the same year mobsters killed some 600 Russian entrepreneurs and attacked the offices of 700 companies in Moscow alone.[31] Between January and October 1996 over fifty bankers were killed in Moscow. According to Moscow police, at least 500 criminal groups operate in the city. Most service businesses pay protection money.[32] The Russian foundation of well-known U.S. philanthropist George Soros has undergone three reorganizations since Soros learned that much of its budget was diverted into "Swiss accounts and luxury cars."[33]

The scale of corruption in postcommunist Russia, unrivaled elsewhere, permeates the entire society, including its top political leaders.

> The theft of the century, perhaps of all time, was that of the Russian energy sector. The assets of the oil giant Gazprom alone are valued in the hundreds of billions of dollars. Although Gazprom and other energy companies were excluded from the official privatization program, 60 per cent stakes in them have ended up, in ways that no one clearly understands, in the hands of a few company insiders, favored politicians, and banks run by the ex-nomenklatura. Among the major shareholders of Gazprom is rumoured to be its former boss Prime Minister Viktor Chernomyrdin. Russia seems to be the only democracy in the world in which the net worth of the prime minister is estimated with a potential error of a few hundred million dollars.[34]

The capital flight out of Russia is, it seems, commensurate to the size of corruption in the country. According to a former U.S. presidential adviser, Zbigniew Brzezinski, since the second half of the 1980s as much as $17 billion out of $86 billion in foreign aid has been "diverted away from intended purposes and recycled to Western banks."[35] Officials from Interpol and the Russian Interior Ministry estimate that Russians hold approximately $300 billion in foreign banks.[36]

Given that the single largest source of investment all over the world is domestic savings and not foreign investment or aid, it follows that Russia's economic growth has been seriously stunted because of the substantial capital flight out of the country. This trend together with organized crime, or the Russian mafia, as it is sometimes called, poses one of the biggest threats to the prosperity of the business community and, therefore, to the emergence and growth of a widespread middle class in Russia.[37] Organized crime in Russia flourishes because law is not enforced and because those responsible for its enforcement are corruptible—a vicious circle that will be difficult to break. Yet without breaking the circle the national economy will not prosper nor will democracy be consolidated. For democracy to function well certain conditions must be met; elimination of large scale corruption, it appears, is one of them: "A Russian elite that combines and confuses criminal, political and entrepreneurial behaviors is a dangerous political laboratory."[38]

A further obstacle to Russia's democracy development is its political police, until recently known under its former abbreviation as the KGB. Yes, the KGB survived the collapse of communism. Albeit its name changed, but very little has changed in its modus operandi. The fact that the Russian "president's own aides cannot speak to one another in confidence for fear of being bugged" demonstrates this clearly.[39] Evidence indicates that the nascent political, economic, and social and cultural institutions in the country continue to be subverted by the political police.[40] Where political police are powerful, civil society is weak, decreasing thereby the chances of a democratic regime surviving in the long run. Although the main function of the former KGB has been to abuse the political, legal, and economic power of postcommunist Russia, the Russian people and politicians, including state leaders, view the political police as something "normal."[41]

That perception alone suggests that Russia's political culture is much different from that of other European countries. For many Russians, a country without the military is as unthinkable as a country without the political police. However, a country with a powerful political police force strengthened by a long tradition of political censorship is hardly a breeding ground for liberal views and attitudes. For a long time Russian society has been divided between Slavophiles, that is, conservatives who cherish Russia's traditional political institutions based on autocracy, and Westernizers, persons who opt for the liberal democracy of the West. Until the fall of communism the Slavophiles or Russian nationalists had the upper hand. Currently the trend is the reverse, but the outcome of the struggle between the two forces is not clear-cut. Polarization between the two opposing worldviews is increasing.

Alexander Solzhenitsyn, a famous former Soviet political dissident and winner of the Nobel Prize in Literature, typifies the Slavophile perspective. He perceives liberalism as hostile to Russian tradition and, for this reason, rejects it. Like many of his compatriots, he opposes party politics, preferring centralization of political power in the hands of one person, a strong ruler or a president. Solzhenitsyn also dislikes the idea of a free market of land and has called for the introduction of an upper limit to the amount of land that an individual can purchase. As nineteenth-century Slavophiles have done, he advocates political and economic isolationism for Russia. In his view, his country has its own, unique road to progress; to copy or even imitate the West in some way will be detrimental to Russia.[42]

The ongoing conflict between continuity and change has been extremely protracted and destructive in Russia's history. One element in Moscow's reforming tradition is the lack of an integrated or comprehensive blueprint for change. The uneven and ad hoc way in which the changes have been implemented leads to confusion and hesitation among the politicians responsible for them and weakens the transformation itself. Hitherto the transformation process has always been unfinished because the persons who initiated it became involved in a political struggle. This stop-and-go pattern of political and economic change has been characteristic of Russia for the last few centuries. Is this time going to be different?

Recent government changes initiated by President Boris Yeltsin suggest that indeed this time it may be different. In March 1997 he replaced most of Russia's conservative ministers, hostile to the continuation of the economic transformation toward a modern market economy, with persons who want to complete the unfinished transformation, like Anatoly Chubais, who pioneered Russian privatization from 1992 to 1995 and was first deputy prime minister until March 1998 when Yeltsin dismissed the entire Chernomyrdin government because of its inefficiency.[43]

In the December 1995 general election the Communist Party of the Russian Federation won about 15.5 million votes, or over one-third of the seats in the lower house of parliament, the State Duma—more than any other party.[44] That result reveals the widespread disillusionment with postcommunist transformation in the country, especially in the rural areas, where the electorate voted overwhelmingly for the communists.

What the Russians experienced since the fall of communism is sometimes described as "shock without the therapy."[45] Whether President Yeltsin, who has no more election campaigns ahead of him, will now prove less of a trimmer is a matter of speculation. So far he has been very prone to changes of mood and policy,[46] and that, in turn, has negatively affected systemic change in the country. The "cliquish" arrangements in politics and economics, often noted by outside observers, frequently are a substitute for policy, and a bad substitute, at that.

Foreigners and the Russians themselves assert that the country's old leveling tradition remains an obstacle to systemic change. Egalitarian values are among those most fostered by them, egalitarianism being very strong in rural areas in particular.[47] Critics debate whether egalitarian values per se are an impediment toward economic transformation. The point is, how are they implemented in practice? The Western practice, "to keep up with the Joneses," is movement up in terms of wealth; in Russia, the practice is usually the reverse: When your neighbor has built a new house and you live in a dilapidated cottage, you will not work harder to get something of similar standard but will burn your neighbour's house so you will be equally poor. This is a strange perception of equality and fails to lead to abundance for all.[48]

With the exception of Poland and perhaps Hungary, trade unions are weak in Eastern Europe, including Russia. This may explain somewhat why unemployment is relatively low in Russia. At the same time, however, this situation has resulted in low wages in Russia so far. Low wages, in turn, do not stimulate higher production, which, as a matter of fact, has significantly decreased since the collapse of communism. The existence of strong trade unions would have strengthened the nascent civil society and consequently resulted in further dispersion of power, thus bolstering the democracy based on it.[49]

Vestiges of the Soviet empire put a brake on Russia's prospects for stable democracy building. Former Soviet imperial institutions such as the armed forces and the military industry have continued to drain Moscow's resources on a scale much higher than in the rest of Eastern Europe. That has been a "specifically Russian hurdle" to systemic change since its outset.[50] Whether this costly and unnecessary impediment toward successful transformation will be in place in the future is difficult to predict.

Another legacy of the past, widely commented upon throughout the world, is the remarkable survival of the Soviet *nomenklatura* in the new, capitalist surroundings. The term *nomenklatura* in Soviet official parlance embraced all top positions in the country requiring formal approval by a special body within the communist party. To become a member of the *nomenklatura* guaranteed an individual high promotion and a *nomenklatura* job for life with all the perks attached to it, and there were many. Such membership was the twentieth-century equivalent of entering the ranks of nobility of the communist realm.

Now, with communism's fall it was widely presumed that new persons, outside the *nomenklatura* circle, would take over political and economic power. That presumption turned out to be wrong altogether. What has happened has been something reminiscent of a theater where actors play various roles in their career; so too in Russia and elsewhere in Eastern Europe persons who previously performed the roles of top communists now act in the new roles of capitalists and democratic leaders. In terms of their personal careers they perform quite successfully. The postcommunist Russian state is still headed by a president who had been a member of the Politburo and the Secretariat, and until March 1998 by a prime minister who had been a member of the party's Central Committee.[51]

There is indeed a striking degree of continuity at leading levels of government in postcommunist Russia: Three-quarters of the presidential administration and nearly three-quarters of the Russian government were former *nomenklatura* members, and among the regional leadership over 80 percent belonged to the *nomenklatura* "club" until recently. Within the Yeltsin political elite as a whole, only one in ten were new to the elite, having started their professional careers in the postcommunist era.[52] By any measure, this is an astounding rate of success during a period of revolutionary metamorphosis. Perhaps as many as two-thirds of the new business elite come from the ranks of the Soviet *nomenklatura*.[53]

Although the goals of democracy and the market economy are in theory separate, in reality they are closely intertwined, success in the latter undoubtedly shoring up the chances of completing the former. Price liberalization, economic stabilization, and privatization of state-owned property are the key steps for introducing the market economy. Price liberalization should balance demand and supply, thereby eliminating queues, which became a hallmark of communism. This, in turn, will bring about economic stabilization. Finally, privatization will result in higher production, greater efficiency, and better-quality consumer goods, ultimately leading to a higher standard of living for the majority of people.

A radical mass privatization program was launched in Russia in late 1992. Although it has relied heavily on privatization vouchers distributed to all citizens, it has also been realized by other means, such as direct sale, public offering, auction, and management-employee buyout.[54] According to official data, in 1995 the private sector accounted for 70 percent of Russia's GDP. By September 1995, a total of 118,000 companies, employing 50 million of the 72 million people in the workplace, had been privatized.[55] In early 1997 approximately 70 percent of firms were partly or fully privately owned.[56]

Initially, the pace of privatization in Russia was rapid. "Some 14,000 [large] companies, an absolutely unprecedented number, were privatized between 1992 and 1994 through a combination of insider buyouts and voucher auctions."[57] As a result, enterprising insiders emerged as majority owners of nearly 70 percent of the country's companies. In addition, over 100,000 small- and medium-sized enterprises were privatized at that time.[58] Although the Russian statistical data are unreliable, they clearly show the scale of ownership change that occurred in Russia since 1992.

It is claimed that by late 1994 Russia managed to overtake Poland and Hungary in privatization,[59] though it started the transfer of property ownership two years later. This in itself is a remarkable achievement. There are presently about 40 million shareholders in Russia.[60] The vouchers the Russians were given as "their share" of the country's economy, worth $40 at the time of issue, dropped in value to $13 within months.[61] By destroying the pillar of communism—state-owned property—Moscow hoped to create capitalism and a market economy at one stroke. Has this goal been achieved? How much has changed since Russian leaders decided to relinquish communism? According to some scholars, at least, "in reality little [has] changed [in Russia]. State monopolies are being transformed into local monopolies—there is little in the way of a real competitive market developing; and little venture capital is being ploughed back into the economy: it goes to Western banks, where it is safe."[62]

One reason some Russian observers think that "little changed" in the country's economy relates to the method used to privatize property. It is occasionally contended that employee buyout amounts in practice to "pseudo-privatization."[63] This, however, is not an issue here. The pertinent question to be asked is whether these enterprises, owned now by employees, will become profitable? If not, will the market economy firmly entrench in Russia? As a rule, former Soviet firms were overemployed. Are they now ready to do the necessary retrenchment to survive without state subsidies?

Empirical evidence gathered so far shows that businesses based on employee-buyout perform worse, often much worse, than newly established private firms. There are several reasons for this. Managers of the employee-buyout companies often do not pursue profit: the overwhelming majority of them consider preserving the workforce and maintaining level of earnings as primary goals. With regard to workers, there is no proof that they "behave in an entrepreneurial spirit rather than being motivated by job security."[64] Whereas minority employee ownership may be beneficial to private companies, majority employee ownership, in all likelihood, may have disastrous results.

By and large minority employee ownership lessens some conflicts of interests between workers and management and makes it easier to restructure a company to make it become profitable and competitive in the market. It also enhances political support for privatization, which at the outset means rather more hardship than benefits. In contrast, majority ownership by employees in privatized firms promotes interest in wages rather than profits and investment. The last thing the worker-owners are interested in is retrenching themselves. Case studies in Russia found no striking difference between the behavior of state-owned enterprises and privatized enterprises. Competition is small. Most companies in the country have adopted a policy of sheer survival.[65] Yet survival is not enough to turn over the bankrupt communist economy into a prosperous capitalist society.

A case study of several hundred recently privatized shops revealed that skills, new skills, may matter more than material incentives with regard to profit making. It follows that new people, who possess skills suitable to a market economy, perform better than old managers, accustomed to command economy rules. The study concluded that "continued control by old managers presents a problem as shareholder oversight over the existing managers" is not effective.[66] There is an urgent need in Russia for "strong owners," usually gained immediately with the direct sale of firms. But purchase of the enterprise by the workers represents at least three-fourths of all privatization completed to date, which bodes ill for the future of the Russian economy. Privatization in the country overwhelmingly creates insider control, not corporate governance by strong outside owners as in the West.

The fact that Russian managers regard preserving the workforce as one of their primary goals explains why unemployment in Russia is relatively low. The important role of the entrepreneur is to take risks, as opposed to the bureaucrat, who avoids risks, instead preferring established routine. Can a bureaucrat be turned into an entrepreneur overnight, if at all? Under what conditions can that aim be realized? Some economists maintain that such change may be achieved through new private enterprises owned by individuals unaccustomed to old habits.

A collectivist habit with regard to property ownership has been most difficult to overcome in one of the most important sectors of the national economy, namely, agriculture. For an economy as a whole to prosper, it must have as one of its main conditions a highly productive agriculture. Yet five years since the inception of the decollectivation program in Russia, privately owned arable land totals approximately 3 to 4 percent of all arable land.[67] During the Soviet era low productive agriculture was a serious obstacle to the country's economic growth, causing the Soviet Union to divert a large part of its foreign currency resources to food imports from the West.

In 1991 individual farmers got the right to lease land or to buy it, but bought land could be sold only after ten years—a rule abolished two years later. The Duma consistently refused to allow full-scale private ownership of land, and it took several years until President Yeltsin introduced private ownership by decree. About 50,000 households entered private farming in 1991; the figure increased to 280,000 in early 1995.[68]

Although the land itself is free by law, the peasants are often charged an application fee of $5 to $50. The average private farm today stands at approximately 40 hectares, the range varing from 2 hectares to 3,500 hectares. That Russian peasants do not measure their success by profit reveals a lot about the conditions of the country's agriculture. Private farming is only semi-monetized. As a general pattern, half of what a farm produces goes to satisfy household requirements and kinship obligations. The remaining half is either sold or bartered. Still, the output of food remains very low, and local food is scarce, expensive, and of poor quality.[69] These are not impressive achievements. Only about two-thirds of Russia's population live in urban areas, and their standard of living is generally higher than that of those who live in the countryside.[70] Therefore to leave one in every three persons outside the economic transformation the country is undergoing today gives a bleak prospect for the future.

What exacerbates the plight of ordinary Russians is the tax system or, rather, the lack of it. Currently only about 20 percent of all taxes are collected and only about 8 percent of federal taxes.[71] Revenues to the federal budget have fallen steadily since 1993. Tax compliance in Russia is worse than in other parts of Eastern Europe.[72] Because taxes in Russia are comparatively high, they provide disincentives rather than incentives for business, and this is why tax avoidance is so widespread. Weak tax law enforcement is highly conducive to this activity. High inflation in the country contributes further to delays in tax collection, since postponement in paying taxes by even by a few months in practice means huge savings for business. This denotes erosion of real tax receipts, which in turn reinforces the government's inclination toward inflationary financing.[73]

Although inflation in Russia is steadily decreasing, going down from over 200 percent in 1994 to just over 20 percent in 1996, it is still high by Western or even Czech standards.[74] It affects the poor more than rich, in this instance the overwhelming majority of the population, causing further disenchantment with economic transformation and a market economy. Under Soviet rule the country experienced neither inflation nor wage arrears, both so widespread nowadays. A presidential commission reported that 62 percent of Russians had not received their wages for September 1996.[75] Some 400,000 unpaid coal miners waited eight months before they went on strike. This fact alone says a great deal about the strength of organized labor and the enforcement of contracts in the country. "Russians are patient," said a Russian worker. "It's all we know."[76]

Russia has the lowest unemployment level among Eastern European countries with the exception of the Czech Republic. Unemployment was completely unknown under the old regime—unknown for political rather than economic reasons, as full employment was one of the communist dogmas complied with until its last days. In reality, however, hidden unemployment existed for many years. With the collapse of communism many unwanted, that is, unsold, products ceased to be produced, and those individuals involved in their production became officially unemployed. Their numbers have contributed to the still-growing unemployment in the country. In mid-1996 the official unemployment in Russia rose to over 9 percent, but the real figure is estimated at over 13 percent.[77]

After domestic savings, foreign investment is nearly everywhere the second largest source of investment. Its role increases greatly in countries devoid of capital and certainly Russia is one such country. Foreign direct investment brings with it modern technology and new management skills, both in short supply in the former communist world. Interestingly, Russia draws little foreign capital despite its potentially huge consumer market because it lacks political stability and infrastructure, whereas lawlessness, corruption, and lax tax legislation are common. This poses an additional barrier to economic development. Per capita investment in the country is only $27, much lower than in most states in Eastern Europe.[78] Since the systemic change started direct foreign investment totals some $5.5 billion, with approximately $1.9 billion in 1995.[79]

What further slows down Russia's economic recovery is its large foreign debt. By the end of 1995, the country's debt reached $124 billion, thus overtaking Brazil as the most heavily indebted country in the world.[80] Merely servicing it requires $20 billion annually. This appeared an impossible task for Russia; in 1994 it paid only $0.9 billion of its debt.

Since 1991 industrial and agricultural production has slumped steadily, by about half. In the first half of 1996 it declined by a further 5 percent, though some Western observers forecast a real growth for 1997 of about 3 percent.[81] Investment is continuing to decline, however. At the time of this writing Russia had not yet joined the World Trade Organization, although it had joined the International Monetary Fund and the World Bank. All these international institutions promote a market economy and competition; hence it would be in Russia's long-term economic and political interest to become a member of the World Trade Organization as soon as possible.

From what has been discussed so far, a mixed picture emerges of an incomplete revolution. Will it be drawn to its ultimate end? This is a matter of speculation. From an individual perspective, the economic transformation of Russia is proving to be a rather slow and painful process, as might be expected taking into consideration its sheer dimensions and its unprecedented novelty in that part of the world. Yet in historical perspective, the scope and pace of fundamental, systemic change in Russia is rapid. Many Russians will not agree with that view, of course; they are impatient, having gone through a revolution of rising expectations and expecting to see palpable, meaningful results of it now. They do not want to wait longer for a rosy future. Instead, they desire to live in comfort today. Their desire for immediate gratification is an important psychological phenomenon, quite understandable, yet difficult to overcome.

Without keeping expectations low, however, continuing systemic change will not be easy. Certainly, a large dose of fairness and justice in implementing the transformation would grossly shore up the chances of a successful completion of it. Alas, this is a sphere of public life that remains most neglected by Russian politicians during the time of the current revolution. The key question concerning the unfinished revolution is a political one: How long will people's tolerance of the pain last, and how resolute will Moscow leaders be in pursuing the revolutionary goals? Are the politicians really willing and able to complete the tasks they embarked upon?

With regard to Russia's future various views are expressed. Some political analysts say that from today's perspective successful liberal democracy is not a foreordained outcome: "History is still open-ended as far as the final outcome of the postcommunist transformation is concerned."[82] Others are of the opinion that either "democracy of default or moderate authoritarianism" is the most likely outcome.[83] Either way, nobody claims that Russia's return to communism is likely. This in itself demonstrates how much Russia has changed in a very short time and is a measure of its success thus far. Although Russia's future remains uncertain, certainly we may say that it will not be Russia as we know it, may we not?

NOTES

1. Theodore Taranovski, "The Problem of Reform in Russian and Soviet History," in Theodore Taranovski (ed.), *Reform in Modern Russian History: Progress or Cycle?* (New York and Cambridge: Woodrow Wilson Center Press and Cambridge University Press, 1995), p. 23.

2. Geoffrey Hosking, "Surviving Communism," *Index on Censorship*, Vol. 25, No. 3, May-June 1996, pp. 39–40.

3. David Remnick, "Can Russia Change?," *Foreign Affairs*, Vol. 76, No. 1, January-February 1997, passim.

4. *The Australian*, 7 March 1997.

5. Ibid.

6. Ibid.

7. Stephen K. Wegren, "Rural Reform and Political Culture in Russia," *Europe-Asia Studies*, Vol. 46, No. 2, 1994, p. 219.

8. Ibid.

9. Thomas Parland, *The Rejection in Russia of Totalitarian Socialism and Liberal Democracy: A Study of the Russian New Right* (Helsinki: Finnish Society of Sciences and Letters, 1993), pp. 33–34.

10. Ibid., p. 34.

11. Taranovski, p. 9.

12. Blair A. Ruble, "Reform and Revolution: Commentary," in Taranovski, p. 411.

13. Taranovski, p. 9.

14. Parland, passim. He argues that "the political and economic structure of the Soviet Union bore the unmistakable mark of its absolutist Muscovite origin" (p. 30).

15. The new constitution gives much power to Russia's president. It is the president who appoints and dismisses cabinet members, including the prime minister.

16. See, for instance, Leon Aron, "Boris Yeltsin and Russia's Four Crises," *Journal of Democracy*, Vol. 4, No. 2, 1993, p. 8.

17. Peter C. Ordeshook, "Russia's Party System: Is Russian Federalism Viable?" *Post-Soviet Affairs*, Vol. 12, No. 3, July-September 1996, p. 214.

18. Jan Zielonka, "New Institutions in the Old East Bloc," *Journal of Democracy*, Vol. 5, No. 2, April 1994, p. 90.

19. Richard Sakwa, "The Struggle for the Constitution in Russia and the Triumph of Ethical Individualism," *Studies in East European Thought*, Vol. 48, Nos. 2–4, September 1996, p. 136.

20. Jyrki Fivonen, "Russian Political Development and Prospects," in Timo Pürainen (ed.), *Change and Continuity in Eastern Europe* (Aldershot, England: Dartmouth, 1994), p. 43.

21. Stephen White, "Post-Communist Politics: Towards Democratic Pluralism?" *Journal of Communist Studies*, Vol. 9, No. 1, March 1993, p. 21.

22. Ibid.

23. Ibid., p. 19.

24. Ninety-three percent of Russians distrust their political parties. Richard Rose, "Postcommunism and the Problem of Trust," *Journal of Democracy*, Vol. 5, No. 3, July 1994, p. 25.

25. Ibid., p. 28.

26. Ibid., p. 19.

27. M. Steven Fish, *Democracy from Scratch: Opposition and Regime in the New Russian Revolution* (Princeton, N.J.: Princeton University Press, 1995), p. 227.

28. Ibid., p. 228.

29. Norman Barry, "The Social Market Economy," in Ellen Frankel Paul, Fred D. Miller Jr., and Jeffrey Paul (eds.), *Liberalism and the Economic Order* (Cambridge: Cambridge University Press, 1993), p. 20.

30. Parland, p. 42.

31. *The New York Times*, 9 November 1996.

32. *The New York Times*, 11 November 1996.

33. *The New York Times*, 17 December 1996.

34. Roman Frydman, Kenneth Murphy, and Andrzej Rapaczynski, "Capitalism with a Comrade's Face," *Transition*, Vol. 2, No. 2, 26 January 1996, p. 8. Another source confirms that scale of corruption in Russia. According to John D Varoli, "Vagit Alekperov, the president of LUKoil, Russia's largest oil company, is believed to have personal assets of $2.4 billion. Viktor Chernomyrdin, the Russian prime minister, is believed to own 1% of Gazprom, which would give him a net worth of 1 billion. Both men supervised the privatization of their companies." See John D. Varoli, "There Are More 'New Poor' than 'New Russians,' " *Transition*, Vol. 2, No. 2, 4 October 1996, p. 7.

35. Zbigniew Brzezinski, "The Stages of Postcommunist Transformation," in Yevhen Bystrycky et al. (eds.), *The Political Analysis of Postcommunism* (Kiev: Political Thought, 1995), p. 112.

36. Varoli, p. 6. See also *Russian Economic Trends*, Vol. 5, No. 2, 1996, p. 7.

37. Justine Burke, "Russia's Curse: Weak Political Institutions Unable to Restrain Arbitrary Leadership," *Demokratizatsya*, Vol. 4, No. 3, summer 1996, p. 339. See also Anders Åslund, "Niektore wnioski z pierwszych czterech lat transformacji," in Marek Dabrowski (ed.), *Polityka gospodarcza okresu transformacji* (Warsaw: PWN, 1995), p. 372.

38. Ken Yowitt, "Undemocratic Past, Unnamed Present, Undecided Future," *Demokratizatsya*, Vol. 4, No. 3, summer 1996, p. 416.

39. J. Michael Waller, "The KGB Legacy in Russia," *Problems of Post-Communism*, Vol. 42, No. 6, November-December, 1995, p. 10.

40. Ibid.

41. Ibid.

42. Parland, pp. 223–229.

43. *The Weekend Australian*, 15–16 March 1997.

44. Mikhail A. Molchanov, "Russian Neo-Communism: Autocracy, Orthodoxy, Nationality," *The Harriman Review*, Vol. 9, No. 3, summer 1996, p. 69.

45. Hosking, p. 42.

46. Robert W. Orttung and Anna Paretskaya, "Presidential Election Demonstrates Rural-Urban Divide," *Transition*, Vol. 2, No. 19, 20 September 1996, p. 33.

47. Wegren, p. 219.

48. Ibid.

49. Åslund, p. 372.

50. Vladimir Kontorovich, "Imperial Legacy and the Transformation of the Russian Economy," *Transition*, Vol. 2, No. 27, 23 August 1996, p. 25.

51. Olga Kryshtanovskaya and Stephen White, "From Soviet Nomenklatura to Russian Elite," *Europe-Asia Studies*, Vol. 48, No. 5, July 1996, p. 729.

52. Ibid., p. 728.

53. The figures vary from source to source. According to Varoli, about 60 percent of Russia's new business elite were either members of the *nomenklatura* or are their children (p. 6). Peter Rutland, however, is of the opinion that "perhaps 65% to 75% of [business] elites" belonged to the *nomenklatura*. See Peter Rutland, "Russia's Unsteady Entry into the Global Economy," *Current History*, Vol. 95, No. 603, October 1996, p. 324.

54. Frydman et al., p. 8.

55. Cited by Rutland, p. 26.

56. Mikhail Zadornov, Chair, Committee on Budget, Taxes, Banks and Finance, Russian Lower House of Parliament (Duma), in a public lecture given at Melbourne University, Melbourne, 25 February 1997.

57. Frydman et al., p. 8.

58. Robert W. Campbell, "Evaluating Russian Economic Reform: A Review Essay," *Post-Soviet Affairs*, Vol. 12, No. 2, April-June 1996, p. 18.

59. *Country Profile: Russia, 1994–1995* (London: Economist Intelligence Unit, 1995), p. 29.

60. Campbell, p. 186.

61. Richard T. De George, "Scientific Capitalism: The Stage after Communism," *Problems of Post-Communism*, Vol. 42, No. 3, May-June 1995, p. 17.

62. Ibid., p. 18.

63. Burke, p. 338.

64. Gabor Hunya, "A Progress Report on Privatisation in Eastern Europe," in Christopher T. Saunders (ed.), *Eastern Europe in Crisis and the Way Out* (London: Macmillan, 1995), p. 287.

65. Ibid., p. 307.

66. Nicholas Barberis, Maxim Boycko, Andrei Shleifer, and Natalia Tsukanova, "How Does Privatization Work? Evidence from the Russian Shops," *Journal of Political Economy*, Vol. 14, No. 4, August 1996, p. 788.

67. Zadornov, lecture. According to other sources, it is slightly higher. Jerry W. Leach contends that private farmers currently hold about 9 percent of the arable land of Russia and claim to produce about 10 percent of the total food supply of Russia. See Jerry W. Leach, "The Emergence of Private Farming in Russia," *Problems of Post-Communism*, Vol. 42, No. 4, July-August 1995, p. 52.

68. Leach, p. 48.

69. Hosking, p. 40.

70. *Country Profile: Russia, 1994–95*, p. 24.

71. Zadornov, lecture.

72. *Russian Economic Trends: Monthly Update*, 22 October 1996, pp. 4–6.

73. Stefan Hedlund and Niclas Sundström, "The Russian Economy after Systemic Change," *Europe-Asia Studies*, Vol. 48, No. 6, September 1996, p. 910.

74. Rutland, p. 322.

75. *The New York Times*, 25 December 1996.

76. Ibid.

77. *Russian Economic Trends*, Vol. 5, No. 2, 1996, p. 8. According to Varoli, "While the official unemployment rate is 3.7% of the potential working population, the International Labor Organization puts unemployment at 8.9%. Yet others say that real unemployment may run as high as 15% to 20%" (p. 11).

78. Natalia Gurushina and Zsofia Szilagyi, "Seeking Foreign Investment in Hungary and Russia," *Transition*, Vol. 2, No. 2, 26 January 1996, p. 24.

79. Rutland, p. 327.

80. Hedlund and Sundström, p. 910.

81. *Country Report: Russia*, 3rd quarter 1996 (London: Economist Intelligence Unit, 1996), p. 882. Brzezinski, p. 117.

83. Fish, p. 229.

4 Poland: Spin-Doctors' State

Poland is a country of paradoxes, myths, and self-illusions and proud of it. At one time or another since the fall of communism, it has had a ministry of privatization that could stop it but not initiate it; it has also had full-time and part-time members of parliament, a trade union that is a political party with deputies in parliament as well as ruling the country since the 1997 general election, and university professors appointed by politicians or academics. This is a country where the term *consistency* is alien to its people and where anarchy has been misinterpreted for centuries as democracy. It is a country that appeared and disappeared from Europe's map several times in its modern political history due to weak governments, a nonexistent standing army, and an outdated economy. It is also a country where political dissent was strongest amidst communist states and where the collapse of communism began. Indeed, the first meaningful attempts to move from a command economy and dictatorial rule to a market economy and democracy were initiated there with partially free parliamentary elections in 1989, soon to be followed by other East European states. It is, too, a country that not only paved the way to the demise of communism in Europe and elsewhere but also contributed, albeit indirectly, to the disintegration of the last imperial power, the Soviet Union.

As time passed by, however, the process of fundamental systemic change in Poland slowed down significantly, and the country was overtaken by other nations, especially the Czech Republic. It took Poland as many as eight years after the process of decommunization began, for instance, to adopt a new, post-Stalinist constitution. This alone speaks volumes about the effectiveness of its political elites and the pace of change itself. Yet since 1989 Poland has undergone a great deal of change encompassing most spheres of public life. Strangely enough, this has often been accomplished despite rather than because of its political leaders, policies, and actions.

Strategically placed between Germany and the former Soviet Union, Poland is the country where World War II broke out. With a population of almost 40 million people, it is a medium-sized European state now lacking a sizeable ethnic minority, which was not the case before the war. Until 1989 it had common borders with three communist states; today it borders seven independent states, for the first time experiencing a change of such magnitude without an international conflict or war. As a matter of fact, Poland's international relations with all its neighbors were never so friendly as they are now. Although Poland has played a significant role in European politics since the Middle Ages it has been little known in the West, in the English speaking countries in particular.

To assert, however, as one of Harvard University's academics does, that "Poland has, without question, one of the deepest democratic traditions of any country in the world"[1] is clearly to mistake anarchy for democracy. Other U.S. academics claim that notwithstanding "an abysmal economy," communist Poland "can produce top-notch economists,"[2] but the economic results achieved by Poland hitherto refute this claim. Many people in Eastern Europe "mouth the words 'market economy' " without necessarily "knowing what they are talking about."[3] Also, to contend that "Poland is the clear trendsetter for the core 'Visegrad' states"[4] comprising the Czech Republic, Slovakia, Hungary, and Poland itself, is to deny reality. Further to maintain that by 1996 Poland "entered a post-transition phase of development"[5] is more wishful thinking than anything else. So is, it seems, to declare Poland a "secure" democracy only seven years after the fall of communism.[6] Since when, one might ask, can a nascent democracy become "secure" in such a short time of only seven years, when an earlier attempt failed after eight years?

These positive misperceptions of Poland are naturally shared by the Poles themselves. To argue, for example, that in the wake of the fall of communism "we [the Poles] are witnessing the second birth of a market economy, democratic polity, and open society"[7] is wrong on all counts. In effect, Poland in its turbulent history has hardly experienced a democracy or market economy. In the modern era the Polish state did not exist from the end of the eighteenth century to the end of World War I. A fragile, multiparty system operated there for only a few years, between 1918 and 1926, to be replaced by a military dictatorship and, in the aftermath of World War II, by communist rule. Economically, it has been a backward country since the Renaissance, experiencing little of modern capitalism and market activity until the collapse of communism toward the end of the twentieth century. The miserable state of the Polish economy, and as its consequence, an impoverished life for a majority of Poles, was vividly described by Poland's Western neighbors, the Germans, as *Polnische Wirtschaft*, a derogatory term denoting a grossly outdated and very inefficient economy run by people who lack business acumen.

Is that going to change today? Will Poland eventually become an economically prosperous country with an entrenched liberal democracy as well? Or, conversely, will it lapse into its political and economic past? It is the argument of this chapter that Poland's prospects for an enduring democracy, albeit not a liberal one, are quite good; it is unlikely, however, that in the foreseeable future the country will establish a well-functioning market economy accompanied by a high standard of living for most of its inhabitants.

When communism fell in Poland in 1989, popular expectations were unrealistically high because the new Polish government "promised half a year of belt-tightening and later marked improvement."[8] Rising economic expectations initially brought a period of social peace at a time of falling incomes, but they also sowed the seeds of future conflicts, when these expectations and promises turned out to be unrealistic.

In two crucial areas Poland performed worse than other countries in Eastern Europe: demonopolization and privatization, the other is the "politics of economic transition."[9] One author goes so far as to contend that by mid-1995 Poland appeared to be in a "serious socio-political crisis."[10] Another commentator came to a similar conclusion even earlier when he stated that "the Polish transition is bordering on the verge of a costly failure."[11]

Yet at the time of the fall of communism in Poland opinions about the country's successful transformation were very different. Western "economists, unlike other outside observers, were and are much less pessimistic about Poland's future [and] were more pessimistic about the developments in the CSSR [Czechoslovakia]."[12] The fact is that by the late 1990s the opposite holds true; that is, economists are now rather more pessimistic about Poland's future, showing that the premises on which earlier conclusions were drawn were false.

To assert that to change "communist laws and political institutions in Poland including the enactment of a new constitution may be [done] over in six months"[13] turned out to be prematurely optimistic. Notwithstanding this inaccurate timetable, the assertion implies that political change, or change in institutions and law, may be attained in a relatively short time. Such change, however, is difficult to achieve in the area of economic transformation unless conditions are ripe for it. They were not in Poland, instead they apparently were in the Czech Republic. Evidently important factors were overlooked or perhaps disregarded during discussions concerning these two countries.

What has not been taken into consideration is the countries' past economic and political performance, not only during the communist period or interwar years but even earlier, going back several centuries. The past matters and usually it is a reliable harbinger of things to come. That is not to say, however, that unexpected occurrences cannot happen but that they are less likely to, otherwise change would not take place at all, which as we all know is not the case.

Further, it is only partially correct to assert that economic transformation itself generates "incentives" not to complete the transformation because all those who can gain by market imperfection will demand it.[14] Empirical evidence does not corroborate this idea totally. A glance at Eastern Europe reveals that systemic economic change in former East Germany and the Czech Republic went much further than in other countries of the region. This denotes that there are other forces at work, forces less visible to observers. These forces relate to competence and familiarity with the market, which reflect on previous economic performance, that is, on economic experience before the imposition of communist rule.

This phenomenon has been noted and commented upon by the Poles themselves. "The pre-communist national traditions were revived and glorified" in the wake of the fall of communism in Poland, stated one observer.[15] This observation supports the notion that people who face new situations resort to a modus operandi familiar to them, that is, one used in the past in similar circumstances. If so, a question arises here concerning the Poles' economic achievements and business performance in times prior to the communist takeover.

Unlike in the Soviet Union, where communism prevailed over three generations, in Poland it lasted for approximately two generations. Thus in the Soviet Union virtually nobody who lived before the Bolshevik seizure of power in 1917 is still alive, in contrast to Poland, where considerable numbers of people who were raised and worked before communism was imposed are still alive. Today these individuals perform the role of "carriers" of past habits and behavior in most spheres of life, the economy and politics included. Because the process of passing tradition from one generation to another is a continuous one that tends to change very slowly over the long term, communist rule in Poland, which lasted less than half a century, failed to destroy completely the country's economic and political traditions.

In attempting to build a democracy and a market economy in their country today, Poles must ask themselves how useful their precommunist tradition is in their efforts to achieve their goals. The answer is that it is of little use if not occasionally a hindrance. When a modern, capitalist economy based on the market emerged and developed in the West, Poland was bypassed. As a consequence, the Poles entered the postcommunist era with little experience of the market. This has been the first hindrance to rapid, successful economic transformation since 1989. In its political past Poland hardly experienced a democracy before, and this fact poses the second hindrance to building a sustainable, long-lasting democracy. This second hindrance is, however, less serious than the other because Poland continues to believe in the myth of a living democratic tradition in the country. Most Poles believe that Poland was a democracy from the sixteenth century to the present, with breaks only when it ceased to exist as a state (1795 to 1918) and when it was under communist rule (1945 to 1989). To disregard strong evidence to the contrary and to nurture the democratic myth helps Poles to establish democracy today. With the collapse of communism, democracy remains the only political system extolled worldwide, and so Poles proudly claim that they have one of the oldest democracies in the world, interrupted twice by outside forces.

The old political regime in Poland, which ceased to exist toward the end of the eighteenth century when Poland was partitioned by its neighbors, was grounded on a veto system. The system degenerated, creating anarchy with concomitant lack of rule of law, inequality, absence of liberty, and widespread corruption. These consequences, seldom noted by the Poles, were frequently observed by foreigners. One of them, who visited the country during its last years of sovereignty in the late eighteenth century contended that "perhaps nowhere is equality and liberty for all more than a day-dream than in Poland, albeit its entire law edifice is built upon and is supposed to stem from them," adding, "There is no law in Poland which could not be broken with money or sustained with it."[16]

In today's Poland, over 200 years later, corruption continues to prevail, equality is a fantasy, and law frequently remains unenforced. Also liberty, so cherished but hardly practised under the old regime, is currently in short supply too. Once Poland was partitioned, the majority of its land and people were incorporated into Russia. This only strengthened corruption, arbitrary rule, and inequality in the country. Only a minority of Poles were affected by Prussian and Austrian political culture because these two states took over much less of Polish territory than did Russia.

In terms of economic development, it also has been observed for centuries that most Poles lived in poverty and that until recently most of the country's national economy was based on agriculture. Following the medieval Christian tradition, Polish nobility and the Polish Roman Catholic Church successfully opposed the emergence of capitalism and a market economy, perceiving trade, interest, and industry as an evil to be fought against. The fight turned out to be victorious for its few winners who benefited from maintaining the status quo, and disastrous for the losers. Will it be different today? Will the majority of Poles benefit this time from the fall of communism? Or will Poland once again plunge into a "serious socio-political crisis," a crisis that, as some argue, appears to have happened already?[17] And will this be followed by anarchy, which is rapidly "approaching," as claimed by others?[18] Such views, are not shared by all observers of the Polish political scene, however. Some observers remain optimistic about Poland's future, maintaining that both democracy and the market will survive and develop despite the weakness and fragility of Poland's governments.[19]

It has been pointed out that the collapse of communism did not create "a systemic vacuum" that can be filled almost at will with another system.[20] To put it differently, some continuity does occur, at least for a while. Is continuity per se a bad thing? Not necessarily. That depends on circumstances. According to the Poles themselves, since the fall of communism they have continued some of their bad habits.[21] They do so because for historical reasons public or civic virtues were never practised by them and, therefore, are unfamiliar to Polish society. The absence of civic virtues is seen by Poles as the most important single obstacle toward building a sustainable democracy and welfare state established on a market economy. Lack of civic virtues favorable to a democracy and economy based on private property and competition stems from the absence of a civil society acting as buffer between the individual and the state.[22]

Between 1989 and 1997, Poland had eight prime ministers. One of them, Jan Krzysztof Bielecki, explained while discussing his country's impediments to developing a liberal democracy and a market economy that his compatriots lacked the civil virtues, competence, and skills necessary to achieve them. He listed among other things a lack of discipline, patience, and long-term planning. In his view, his fellow Poles prefer small but immediate gain, often short-lived, to a large but distant one, frequently of lasting endurance. This attitude has been coupled with a lack of organizational skills and critical thinking. The Poles' lack of self-criticism has led them to "believe that they know how [capitalism and a market economy] can be built."[23] Hitherto achieved results, however, do not easily inspire confidence in their optimism.

In explaining the Polish national character, a well-known Polish author contended that lack of accountability was one cause of Poland's economic backwardness. In his opinion, Poles also lack responsibility and are insubordinate and unreliable.[24] Furthermore, such civic virtues as tolerance, compromise, and mutual respect are by and large absent in Poland.[25] Without these virtues, however, creating a liberal society in any meaningful sense of that word will be extremely difficult. It has been often observed that in the public arena Poles usually pursue their special narrow interests in nearly complete disregard of national interests or the common good.

The Roman Catholic Church in Poland is a good example of this attitude. Under communist rule the Church struggled against religious and political discrimination quite effectively, having no counterpart in the Soviet bloc. For its effective opposition the Church was highly appraised by the Poles, the overwhelming majority of them being Roman Catholics. Yet with the demise of communism, the Church drastically changed its position and is now a "tower of intolerance."[26] That change, in turn, has divided Polish society almost equally and, most likely, has contributed significantly to the leftist party's success in the 1993 parliamentary elections and the 1995 presidential elections.

Thus, as it turned out, the Church's views on social matters such as abortion had serious political implications, resulting in a polarized society. From the perspective of democracy building, that may be a positive factor because it is conducive to the creation of a multiparty system based on a variety of ideas, views, policies, and ideologies instead of a system characterized by personalized politics wherein political leaders struggle for power for power's sake. In the wake of the collapse of communism came personalization of the party and electoral systems and thereby personalization of Poland's public life. With the Catholic Church's involvement in politics— for instance, in the discussion of the proposed text of a new constitution— the Poles became less concerned with personalities and more concerned with opinions. This has been a healthy process as far as political pluralism is concerned, but it has not been an exercise in tolerance and accommodation.

For compromise to prevail, it is not enough to realize that today's election winners might be tomorrow's losers, that restraint is required on the side of the rulers, who in return would expect the same when they become the opposition. It goes deeper, to what we understand as truth—whether there exists one ideal truth, ever-lasting, or it varies from age to age depending on our knowledge of ourselves and the outside world. It also needs empathy for other people's feelings and values—something the Roman Catholic Church in Poland has been devoid of throughout its history, and this has left a lasting impact on the Poles' behavior in the public domain, and in politics in particular. In that respect there is plenty of room for the Poles to learn from the older, Western democracies.

Furthermore, the future of an enduring democracy in the country hinges to a certain extent on its ability to attain meaningful economic success, since for many individuals in Poland the yardstick used to evaluate the systemic changeover to democracy is "economic effectiveness."[27] If palpable economic achievements are not felt by ordinary Poles after a while, then the attraction of democracy will be greatly reduced. In such a situation resort to authoritarian rule will become more than a mere possibility.[28] One of the most popular historical figures in present-day Poland is Marshal Jozef Pilsudski, a person who used military force to overthrow a democratically elected government, introducing in its place a military dictatorship that lasted from 1926 to the outbreak of World War II. Many Poles perceive Pilsudski as a strong and effective politician, and they long for such a personality to appear again. The likelihood of its occurring in the foreseeable future is, from today's perspective, negligible.

After World War II, Pilsudski's military rule was superseded by communist rule, thus postponing the reappearance of a multiparty system until 1989. Because political dissent in Poland was strong and widespread in the last decade before communism collapsed many people expected that the process of party formation and development would be easy. This expectation was largely wrong: The process of party formation and development was in effect protracted; it got off to a particularly slow start and encountered more hurdles in Poland than it did in most other countries of Eastern Europe.[29] A first fully free general election was held as late as October 1991, over two years after the partially free election of June 1989. The election of 1991 produced a fragmented parliament with twenty-nine political parties represented in it. The fragmentation led, as might be expected, to considerable problems in producing a stable, effective, and lasting government. By 1993 the number of registered political parties reached 222.[30] As a result of the fragmentation of parliament, all governments in Poland have been hitherto coalition governments. They were also of short duration until 1993 when an electoral law based on an unrestricted proportional system was changed and a 5 percent threshold was introduced for parties to be represented in the Sejm or lower house. Consequently, the 1993 general election resulted in reducing the number of parties in the Sejm from twenty-nine to six. This stabilized the Polish political scene considerably by producing a coalition government consisting of two parties only that lasted throughout the entire term of office. In the 1997 general election, five parties overcame the 5 percent threshold.

Surprisingly to many people, the parties that received the largest number of votes in the 1993 election and formed a government were those that had run the country since the communist takeover in the aftermath of World War II, namely, the reformed and renamed communist party and the peasant party. Two years later, in December 1995, a leader of the ex-communist party, Aleksander Kwaśniewski, replaced Lech Wałęsa, a symbolic figure in the struggle against communism, as president of Poland.

A Poland overtaken by leftist political forces suggests a society undergoing a change of basic values. Until December 1995 Poland was regarded as deeply Catholic and highly anticommunist; hence the political turnaround was unanticipated. Such a prospect had been seen as a remote possibility disregarded by most people in the West and in Poland itself. Thus far, however, the resurgence of the left has helped Poland avoid the violent conflict seen elsewhere in postcommunist Eastern Europe and is undoubtedly a sign of democratic progress as successive governments have accepted the fact of parliamentary defeat and the postcommunist parties returned constitutionally to power. This does not mean, of course, that Poland's political development and the institutional fate of its major parties are now complete.

Among the countries of Eastern Europe, Poland was probably weakest in the process of party development, and it appears that the emergence of a stable multiparty system in the country would be an arduous one. The 1993, 1995, and 1997 election results indicate that the Polish electorate is profoundly divided along ideological lines, which obviously is hardly conducive to political stability, consensus-building, and constructive opposition.[31] From that it follows that the Polish political scene is not yet a fertile ground for liberal values to take root.

Since the takeover of authority in Poland was negotiated by noncommunists with government officials representing the old regime, unlike in several other East European states, former communists have preserved much power. The takeover was a process rather than an abrupt event, and though executed peacefully it left a lot of resentment among many ordinary Poles, who believed at the time of the power takeover that it would be complete and last forever. They hardly expected that the persons who would profit most from privatization of state-owned property would be members of the notorious *nomenklatura*, or former communist elite, rather than former political dissidents. "For the Poles," writes a Western commentator, "it is difficult to understand why the results of democracy and the defeat of communism means that those who lived well in the past now have it even better, and those who were oppressed by them should be worse off than before."[32]

Moreover, real and effective decommunization or screening, though much debated, has not been introduced in Poland, unlike elsewhere, as in the Czech Republic. To undergo fundamental systemic change without dealing with the justice system has taken many Poles by surprise, for justice appears to lie at the heart of democratic polity. Is it possible, one may ask, to attain democracy without justice? According to successive postcommunist governments in Poland, the answer is yes.

That view was declared publicly by Tadeusz Mazowiecki, prime minister of the first noncommunist-led coalition government. In his maiden speech in the Sejm he declared that communist officials would not be investigated for past misdeeds thereby implying that they would be eligible to exercise the highest positions of authority in the country if elected.[33] Like Mazowiecki, several other Polish prime ministers have opposed administering justice despite having been themselves oppressed by the communist regime not so long ago. To many people, that unexplainable position was most strongly defended by Adam Michnik, also a former political dissident. In his opinion, justice with regard to communists in practice denotes "revenge," which he opposes on humanitarian grounds. Instead, he proposed "compassion." For him, "The most reasonable position must be: give priority to compassion and let justice follow."[34]

How long should it take for justice to "follow"? According to Michnik, "50 years." He wrote: "As for the [political police] archives, they should remain sealed for 50 years, in order that no politician can be in a position to draw on them while fighting his political battles."[35] Perhaps it is because the police archives were sealed, as recommended, that an alleged former Soviet and Russian political police informer, Józef Oleksy, succeeded in becoming Poland's prime minister. After accused of being a KGB informer, Oleksy resigned, only to be elected leader of the largest then party in the Sejm, the ex-communist party. The Oleksy affair reveals that the concept of justice has not put down strong root in Polish society, most likely as a result of its undemocratic past.

What justice means in Poland sharply contrasts with what it means to Poland's western and southern neighbors, namely, the Germans and the Czechs. A former East German political dissident complained that following the demise of communism in his country, he expected justice to be done. To his surprise, it did not happen. "We wanted justice," he said. "Instead we got the rule of law."[36] The Poles, however, have neither the rule of law nor justice.

After the fall of communism the decommunization bill was passed in the Czech parliament. Former *nomenklatura* were excluded from top government positions for several years and restitution was made of property nationalized by the communists. Vaclav Havel, also a former political dissident and later president of the Czech Republic, in a conversation with Adam Michnik completely disagreed with Michnik's approach to the issue of justice. For Havel, "The need to administer justice, is clearly justified and natural"; it has nothing to do with revenge, as these two notions are not synonymous.[37] Havel contends that as far as justice is concerned, "Society needs some public action in this regard because otherwise it would feel that the revolution remains unfinished."[38] Referring to Michnik's idea of compassion as an ersatz of justice, he said: "As a state official I have no right to pronounce an act of grace for everyone."[39] His position on this issue is contrary to that taken by Mazowiecki.

Only in 1997 was a law passed in Poland to require prospective and current public officials to declare whether they had collaborated with the secret police prior to the collapse of communist rule. Strangely enough this law was introduced by the former communist party and not by its opponents. Whether the law will work is very doubtful because sufficient time has elapsed since the collapse of communism to destroy secret police documents detrimental to communist party members. Furthermore, strictly speaking this is not a screening law: State institutions are not required to initiate investigations into whether present or prospective officials collaborated with the political police before 1989. The officials themselves are required to "confess" about their infamous past. This law thus fails to exclude former *nomenklatura* members from holding top government positions for a certain period.

The issue of justice in Poland is related to morality. Some scholars argue that the collapse of communism was, above all, a "moral" collapse. The communist command economy was unproductive because it is "immoral." In their opinion, efficiency is part of morality. "If one does not organize society morally, one is unlikely to succeed in organizing it materially."[40] If that view is correct, then a replacement of one immoral regime by another in Poland is a bad omen for the country's economic recovery. Where there is no justice, rule of law can hardly exist; and if it does not, which is the case presently in Poland, corruption is rife.

According to public opinion polls in Poland from the mid-1960s to early 1990s, few people consider bribery a symptom of "negative social deviation," as is the case in the West.[41] One out of every five respondents admitted to having given or accepted a bribe. Almost all Poles have the general impression that corruption in their country is extremely widespread.[42]

If this is so, the question arises, is corruption bad because it makes a mockery of the principle of equality before the law or because it has economic consequences as well? There is no doubt that corruption increases the costs of contracts and deals, thereby lowering the standard of living of ordinary people. It may result in a monopoly and thus further decrease the people's standard of living. Corruption ultimately perpetuates an ineffective economic system by eliminating competition. Without competition, the national economy, whatever it is, is not a market one based on the law of demand and supply, which leads to competition, declining prices, and in consequently a higher standard of living.

Corruption is an unmistakable proof that absent in postcommunist Poland is the rule of law, including tax law, so important for any national economy and even more so for an economy in crisis. Although tax law in Poland is not as widely abused as in Russia, nonetheless it is far from being efficient and thoroughly enforced. Poland's former president, Lech Wałęsa, for instance, who received $1 million for a copyright to make a movie based on his book, declared that he would not pay the $120,000 tax levied on his earning—and he did not.[43] On official state voters' pamphlets, Aleksander Kwaśniewski, who succeeded Wałęsa as president gave false information concerning his education. Misrepresentation on the pamphlets is a felony under U.S. law, punishable in the state of Oregon with a maximum of five years in prison and a $100,000 fine.[44] It is not so in Poland. More significant, Kwaśniewski's deceit did not prevent his winning the presidential election. This alone tells much about Polish politicians and even more about their electorate: It reveals that Poland's political elites are above the law and, it appears, that the voters accept this; otherwise they would not have elected Kwaśniewski to the presidency, which they did while being well aware that he had lied to them.

The Polish electorate seems to be more concerned with economic issues than political ones. Perhaps this is why the country failed to adopt a new constitution until eight years after the fall of communism. "First deal with the economy, then with politics" may be the Poles' unspoken assumption in this regard, as though these two could be separated without a negative effect on either. Empirical evidence refutes this assumption, however. The question was posed, would the adoption of a new constitution enhance the prospects for economic transformation in the course of a simultaneous political and economic systemic change? Evidence gathered from twenty-five postcommunist countries demonstrates that postponement of the adoption of a new constitution "does not appear to advance the process of economic reform when considered against the experiences of the postcommunist countries."[45] To the contrary, new constitutions do appear to contribute to the political capacity to "adopt economic reform measures."[46]

In other words, politics has an impact on the economy, and the impact of constitutions dating to communist times is negative in terms of economic change; the opposite holds true in the case of newly adopted constitutions—which, one may add, is not unexpected. Furthermore, a reason to change from a communist constitution to a democratic one, based on recognition of private property, is to stimulate economic transformation in order to achieve meaningful economic growth and ultimately an affluent society. This crucial point has been missed since 1989 by the Polish parliament, which has shown signs of descending into immobility, impotence, and almost irrelevance. That it took nearly a decade to produce a new constitution is a case in point.

Instead of swiftly passing a new constitution shortly after the collapse of communism, the Sejm amended the old constitution, doing so in such a way as to make unclear the role of the president and the resposibilities of the government rule. That lack of clarity has led to a nearly constant struggle between the president and the prime minister, resulting in frequent changes of government. It has personalized Polish politics on a scale unencountered elsewhere in the region. It has, in short, been detrimental to the consolidation of the nascent democracy and the emerging market economy. During Kwaśniewski's presidency the situation has improved greatly, although a constitutional solution was still urgently needed to clarify the functions of governmental leaders and governing bodies.

The first few governments in postcommunist Poland had their origin in Solidarity, an independent trade union established under the old regime, in 1980. Because of Solidarity, Poland has experienced little worker unrest since 1989. Workers expected those who came to power thanks to worker support to be sympathetic to their demands. Consequently, labor protests in the country tended to be isolated and containable. Poland experienced little violent or uncontrolled labor disruption. Attempts by radical labor organizers to generate a broader protest movement against radical transformation consistently failed. Initially, the living standards of many Poles fell, but several years later they were on the rise, though not affecting everyone the same. This, coupled with the perception of postcommunist governments as legitimate, weakened the labor movement and so resulted in relative social peace.[47] Besides being a trade union Solidarity is also a political party with deputies in the Sejm. This gives it an opportunity to express its views in parliamentary debates and to defend workers' interests as it sees them. Probably, as a consequence of it, political stability in the country is enhanced.

Yet at the outset of the demise of communism several successive Polish neo-liberal governments allowed the social safety net to disintegrate nearly completely at a time when unemployment emerged and mounted rapidly, reaching 15 percent in 1995; largely because of high unemployment they were voted out of office. They were replaced by the former communist party, which in coalition with the peasant party, was perceived by the electorate as a better advocate of its material interests.[48] To neglect the interests of the people most negatively affected by the party's policies turned out to be politically costly to the neo-liberals and detrimental to the process of systemic transformation. The leftist government formed in 1993 considerably slowed down privatization and other measures undertaken to introduce a market economy in the country. Instead of rapidly proceeding with systemic change, Polish neo-liberals unnecessarily delayed it; however, to delay painful but unavoidable economic transformation ultimately makes things worse for the poor.[49] Whether the post-1997 election coalition government, led by Solidarity in alliance with the Freedom Union, will accelerate the pace of privatization and a market-oriented change is uncertain.

In Poland, failure to resolve the poverty and safety net issues, among other things, has threatened to derail economic transformation and also jeopardized the nascent democracy. Efficiently executed social security policy can reduce poverty and help to sustain support for economic change, thereby fostering democracy. Unresolved social security problems in Poland, however, were cushioned by dissent among the trade unions. In addition to Solidarity there exists in the country a trade union established by the communist authorities prior to 1989, but virtually no trade unions have been formed in the private sector since the command economy ceased to exist. Although this weakens the trade union movement, it strengthens social peace in the country.

What further enhances social peace is the relatively successful protection of the standard of living of old-age pensioners compared to other social groups. Together with disability pensioners the aged make up a sizeable part of Polish society. Rather well organized and vocal, they have managed better than many other people to protect their material interests. Because voter participation among the aged is high, their interests are looked after by various political parties competing for pensioner support.[50] In turn this political support contributes to strengthening social peace in Poland even more. Certainly, to move from dictatorship to democracy is greatly facilitated when social conflicts are rare, at least at the outset of systemic transformation. This gives the politicians an opportunity to deal with other political and economic issues.

It could also be argued that the absence of ethnic minorities in Poland is conducive to the establishment of a democracy. Before World War II Poland had political problems involving its several large ethnic minorities. In the aftermath of the war, Poland emerged virtually without significant ethnic minorities, who made up only 2 percent of its population. When communism collapsed in the country, ethnic conflict did not occur, as it did elsewhere, for instance, in Yugoslavia or the former Soviet Union. It is sometimes contended that ethnic conflict feeds authoritarian tendencies and almost always makes it difficult for democracy to emerge and to consolidate.[51] Vice versa, in countries that have no serious ethnic cleavages, democracy building has progressed further and has better chances of survival in the long run.

Apparently there is a direct link between ethnic conflict and nondemocratic development in Eastern Europe. Often in ethnically divided societies majority and minority are fixed rather than fluid; hence in such circumstances majority rule is more a problem than a solution because it results in domination without a foreseeable end. Domination generates resistance; then usually there appear political leaders who pursue conflict rather than accommodation, hoping to profit from it. Thus for Poland to have no politically meaningful ethnic minority today is a considerable advantage in its efforts to establish a sustainable democracy.

Possessing initial conditions favorable to democracy creation is not tantamount to ultimate success, namely, the establishment of an enduring democratic polity. As stated earlier, success hinges on the economic performance of the postcommunist regime. The command economy in Poland, as elsewhere, was based on four dogmas—state ownership of property, monopoly, full employment, and fixed prices—which made the country's economic functioning highly inefficient, to put it mildly. To turn the economy into a very productive one, the opposite is required, that is to say, private ownership, competition, and liberalization of prices with the unavoidable unemployment as its consequence, at least in the initial stage of transformation. Unemployment is unavoidable initially for a variety of reasons, one of them that under the old regime factories produced goods for which there was no demand. To stop production, however, results in dismissal of workers who produced these unwanted commodities and thereby creates unemployment.

Hitherto economic results achieved by Poland are of a mixed character. In terms of privatization, one of the most important indicators of economic change, in 1996 the country lagged well behind the Czech Republic, Hungary, Estonia, and Lithuania. At the end of 1995, slightly over 40 percent of large enterprises were privatized in Poland, whereas in Russia over 60 percent were privatized, in Lithuania and Hungary nearly 80 percent, in the Czech Republic about 90 percent, and in Estonia close to 100 percent.[52] By the end of August 1996, out of 8,000 large state enterprises, only 171 were sold. Approximately half of all those enterprises were leased, turned into worker-management joint ventures, or liquidated.[53] Six years after Poland's economic transformation began, the private sector produced over half of the GDP and employed just over 60 percent of the workforce.[54] These figures are not impressive, not only in comparison with other East European states but also with Poland's performance a few years earlier. Already in March 1993 the private sector in Poland accounted for over 58.0 percent of overall employment including agriculture and for 44.5 percent without it.[55] These figures become even less impressive if one takes into account that in Poland, unlike elsewhere, most arable lands (about 75 percent in 1989) were privately owned under communist rule.

Also, it should be noted that Polish statistics, like Russia's, are unreliable. What inflated the data concerning the size of the private sector in postcommunist Poland was reclassification of cooperatives from the state sector to the private one.[56] The sharp decline in output and employment in the state-owned sector, too, resulted in a relative growth of the private sector.

From 1990 to 1993, the private sector created 3.5 million new jobs. Private firms employed 45 percent of the nonagricultural labor force in Poland in 1993. In retail trade the private sector employed over 90 percent of workers and in construction more than three-quarters.[57] It appears that the development of small- and medium-sized enterprises and the spread of entrepreneurial activity were far more important than privatization of state enterprises in moving Poland away from a command economy.[58]

From the onset of systemic change privatization in Poland was politicized in favor of safeguarding worker and former *nomenklatura* benefits. A great majority of state-owned firms have been leased by employee companies and former *nomenklatura* members. The so-called *nomenklatura* privatization, regardless of justification on purely economic grounds, clearly violates the principles of equity and justice. Little wonder that some people refer to privatization in Eastern Europe, including Poland, by quoting Pierre Joseph Proudhon's statement that "property is theft."[59] The ambivalent nature of the law system in Poland in general and the loopholes in its tax law and customs regulations in particular enabled big fortunes to be made quickly in Poland after 1989.

The emerging pattern of privatization, which started with radical rhetoric, seems to increasingly display features of the gradual approach, especially since the election of 1993, when ex-communists formed a coalition government and the pace of privatization slowed down significantly in Poland. Even earlier, though at the onset of fundamental change, the privatization ministry in Poland, ostensibly established to promote it, could not initiate privatization but only approve or disapprove the privatization proposals submitted to the ministry by firms themselves.[60] Apparently even this modest step toward privatization was too much for the leftist coalition government, which decided to dissolve it altogether.

Not surprisingly, seven years after the initiation of economic transformation, approximately 40 percent of the GDP was still produced by state-owned firms.[61] In reality, however, that official figure may be somewhat lower, since statistics in Poland do not include illegal or undetected—and thus untaxed—economy, which is estimated to be quite large, producing approximately 25 to 30 percent of GDP in 1994.[62] All this reveals that the Polish state remains a powerful economic figure indeed, the most powerful in the country, and that law and order are poorly enforced. To be so powerful economically in a state largely missing law and order is a serious impediment to establishing sustainable democracy. It is also an important obstacle to economic recovery, since state-owned firms are generally less productive than privately owned ones. Successive Polish governments, however, have expressed little concern about it or the policies they pursue. A Polish minister of industry once stated, "No industrial policy is the best industrial policy."[63] That statement says much about the economic competence of the Polish political elite.

To slow down economic transformation was an official goal of the Polish Peasants' Party. Its leader, a former Polish prime minister, Waldemar Pawlak, said that his "party is putting a brake on the reforms and will

deliberately continue to do so."[64] This approach to economic transformation, taken to protect the interests of the peasants more than anybody else,
has not yet worked. As a matter of fact, total agricultural production in
Poland declined between 1989 and 1995 by about 9 percent. At the same
time the number of persons who work exclusively in agriculture increased
by more than 13 percent.[65] Whereas in Western Europe only 5 percent of
the workforce is employed in agriculture, in Poland that figure is over five
times higher.[66] Hidden unemployment in the agricultural sector is estimated
to be about 1.5 million people. Polish agriculture, which employs 26 percent
of the total workforce, produced less than 7 percent of the GDP in 1995.[67]
In that year peasants' incomes were on average 40 percent lower than in
1989.[68]

Throughout communist rule Poland was the only country in the Soviet
bloc where most arable lands were privately owned. Although this was
advantageous then, since productivity was higher in privately owned farms
than in state ones, after the collapse of communism this beneficial factor
disappeared. Most Polish farms are small; the average size is less than 7
hectares. Today to achieve high productivity and profit large-scale farms
are needed. Yet Polish peasants and their party defended, quite successfully,
the status quo. In the Czech Republic, which lacked private farms under the
old regime, the newly created private farms are large-scale to boost productivity and profits. Between 1989 and 1995 the number of Czechs employed
in agriculture was halved to 7 percent of the total workforce.[69] In 1993 an
average-sized farm owned by a Czech was 1,408 hectares, that is, over 200
times greater than its Polish equivalent.

Peasants with land under 5 hectares represent the most numerous category in Poland, accounting for half the total land managed by them. Peasants
with farms larger than 50 hectares are a negligible presence in terms of both
numbers and area. By 1994, that is, in five years, only 2 percent of
state-owned farms were privatized (and 33 percent were leased). Whereas
Czech agriculture is little protected by the state, in Poland the situation is
different. Suffice it to say, that through higher customs, agricultural products are much better protected from foreign competition than are industrial
products, with a ratio of 4 to 1 in favor of the former.[70] The end result of
sustaining outdated, inefficient, and poorly productive agriculture is a high
price for the product and a lower standard of living for nearly all Poles.
Further, the more consumers are required to spend on food, the less money
they spend on manufactured goods. Of course, this is a disincentive for the
economy to expand, especially for industry and services. It means also that
less money is saved, and therefore there is less domestic capital for invest-

ment, so badly needed now. Evidence shows that domestic savings are the biggest single source of investment worldwide. It follows that if a country is to attain a high rate of economic growth, its agricultural products should be cheap. The low level of domestic savings in Poland is insufficient for sustaining rapid economic growth. The rate of savings in the country is currently about 17 to 18 percent of GDP, whereas in Southeast Asia, for instance, it is 50 percent higher.[71]

The second largest source of investment, although much lower than that derived from domestic savings, is foreign capital. Between late 1990 and the end of 1997 foreign investment in Poland reached approximately $20.6 billion, meaning that Poland has overtaken Hungary as the country in the region with the largest foreign investment.[72] In per capita terms, however, foreign direct investment in the country was significantly lower than in several other Eastern European states. At the end of 1994 it was $691 in Hungary, $300 in the Czech Republic, $291 in Estonia, and only $114 in Poland.[73] And as of mid-1996 it stood at $265 compared with $1,299 in Hungary and $586 in the Czech Republic.

Potentially Poland has a much larger consumer market than all other former communist states with the exception of Russia and Ukraine. Its population doubles that of Hungary and the Czech Republic combined, and yet Poland has failed to attract much foreign investment thus far. What prompted Western investors to withhold from making substantially large investments in Poland? Apparently the causes are political as well as economic. Frequent changes of governments and their policies in the first four years following the collapse of communism brought about political instability that deterred foreign investors. Also, the lack of adequate communication and transport system, as well as a developed banking and financial sector keeps foreign investors away. These discouraging conditions for investment have been reinforced by government bureaucracy, indecision, and hesitation.[74] Yet in 1996 and 1997 Poland received more in terms of foreign direct investment than any other Eastern European country.

Foreign investment means not only the import of modern technology and managerial skills but also the creation of new jobs. New jobs are much needed because unemployment in Poland is high; in mid-1996 it was above 14 percent, or nearly 2.5 million persons.[75] It decreased to 12.8 in July 1997. The relatively high cost of labor deters foreign investment in the country and thereby contributes to a high level of unemployment. Although wages in Poland remain low, labor cost is high because social security, or health and old-age pension expenses, is covered entirely by the employer,[76] which makes Poland unique in this respect.

In addition, there is mounting pressure in Poland to use disability and early retirement pensions as covert unemployment benefits. This step is politically expedient, because pensions are generally higher than unemployment benefits; yet this step would decrease the standard of living of people who are still employed and pay somewhat higher taxes in order to support those who do not work any more. The total number of persons unemployed and those who are on disability and old-age pensions doubled between 1989 and 1995 in relation to those who are in the workforce.[77] The real number of unemployed is probably significantly lower than the official figure because some people who receive the dole are working.

As a result of several economic and political changes introduced soon after the collapse of communism, Poland's national economy is currently emerging from the crisis in which it was immersed from 1989 to 1991. In 1992 it began to recover; its GDP grew by 2.6 percent in that year and increased to nearly 7 percent in 1995, just over 6 percent in 1996, and 7 percent in 1997.[78] Whether this level of economic growth will be sustained over the long term is uncertain. The economic policy of a leftist coalition government was less conducive to economic growth than its predecessor. Since 1993, when the ex-communists took over the government, Poland has been moving down on a list of countries ranking economic freedom. According to the Heritage Foundation, Poland was number 85 in terms of economic freedom in 1996, well behind the Czech Republic, which was ranked 11, and behind another five former communist states.[79] In fact, Poland was listed under the category of countries labeled as generally unfree economically. It is therefore not surprising that in 1995 the country's GNP was still below its 1989 level.[80]

The political and economic transformation of the communist system in Poland has been critically constrained by lack of organizational flexibility and capacity for institutional change. Furthermore, without a total revolution, there is no clear-cut break with the old order. Half measures undertaken so far will not result in self-sustaining economic development in the long run.

None of the postcommunist governments have succeeded in eliminating inflation, which in 1989 reached 585 percent; and though it was reduced below 22 percent by 1995 and 13.2 percent at the end of 1997, it remains high by international standards.[81] Poland's hyperinflation in 1989 was just the fourth occurrence of its kind in world history. Poland has the dubious honor of being the second country to suffer hyperinflation twice.[82]

Certainly, inflation diminishes the standard of living of most people affected by it. What helps to stop it from declining even further is a cross-border trade between Poland and its seven neighbors. Unintended, unplanned, and mostly uncontrolled, the trade contributes significantly to the country's national economy in terms of hard currency reserves, production, and employment. Such spontaneously developed economic activity gives good insight into the advantages of the emergence of a market economy undisturbed by the politicians.

Yet not to intervene at all in market functioning is not the best economic policy. Experience shows that the best economic policy is to intervene into market operations, but doing so that such economic development, not economic decline, is stimulated. True, it is easier said than done and it requires generations to acquire the necessary skills and practical experience. That skill and experience are what most ordinary Poles are still lacking, and their politicians are by and large unaware of it.

To conclude, Poland's efforts to relinquish communism and to build in its place a democracy and a market economy have hitherto not been so bad as some of Poland's detractors claim and not so impressive as some admirers assert. "To speak of a Polish private-sector miracle"[83] is an obvious exaggeration, but so is the claim that Poland is in a "serious socio-political crisis."[84] In terms of the scope and pace of its economic transformation Poland is not a leading country in Eastern Europe, but neither is it the last one. Although much more remains to be done to firmly establish a market economy in Poland, when one takes into account the state of the Polish economy prior to the downfall of communism, in the last two centuries or so, the results attained since 1989 are not so poor but rather more or less as expected.

With regard to political transformation Poland is performing better than in the economic sphere. Of course, when there is a will, systemic change is easier to achieve in politics than in economics, and it appears that there is a great deal of will in today's Poland. This, together with the survival of the myth of a democratic past, considerably increases Poland's chances of achieving a sustainable democracy. Yet the country has a long way to go to turn it into a liberal regime. For this to occur in a country whose modern history is alien to the idea will not be easy in the short run. What it will be in the long run remains to be seen.

NOTES

1. Jeffrey Sachs, *Poland's Jump to the Market Economy* (Cambridge, MA: MIT Press, 1993), p. 112.

2. John Clark and Aaron Wildavsky, *The Moral Collapse of Communism: Poland as a Cautionary Tale* (San Francisco: ICS Press, 1990), p. XIII.

3. James Millar, "From Utopian Socialism to Utopian Capitalism: The Failure of Revolution and Reform in Post-Soviet Russia," in Timo Pürainen (ed.),

Change and Continuity in Eastern Europe (Aldershot, England: Dartmouth, 1994), p. 13.

4. Elizabeth Pond, "Poland Is Not Yugoslavia. Neither Is Ukraine," *The Harriman Review*, Vol. 8, No. 2, July 1995, p. 4.

5. Ray Taras, "The End of the Wałęsa Era in Poland," *Current History*, Vol. 95, No. 599, March 1996, p. 128.

6. *Newsweek*, 9 December 1996, p. 17.

7. Piotr Sztompka, "The Intangibles and Imponderables of the Transition to Democracy," *Studies in Comparative Communism*, Vol. 24, No. 3, September 1991, p. 295.

8. Jan Winiecki, "The Polish Transition Programme: Underpinnings, Results, Interpretations," *Soviet Studies*, Vol. 44, No. 5, 1992, pp. 812–813.

9. Ibid., p. 832.

10. Andrzej Korbonski, "How Much Is Enough? Excessive Pluralism as the Cause of Poland's Socio-Economic Crisis," *International Political Science Review*, Vol. 17, No. 3, July 1996, p. 300.

11. Winiecki, p. 833.

12. Barbara Krug, "Blood, Sweat, or Cheating: Politics and the Transformation of Socialist Economies in China, the USSR, and Eastern Europe," *Studies in Comparative Communism*, Vol. 24, No. 2, June 1991, p. 144.

13. Sztompka, p. 310.

14. Krug, p. 148.

15. Piotr Sztompka, "Looking Back: The Year 1989 as a Cultural and Civilizational Break," *Communist and Post-Communist Studies*, Vol. 29, No. 2, June 1996, p. 126.

16. Fryderyk Schulz, *Podróże Inflantczyka z Rygi do Warszawy i po Polsce w latach 1791–1793* (Warsaw: Czytelnik, 1956), p. 124 and p. 135, respectively.

17. For instance, by Korbonski, p. 298.

18. For example, by Grzegorz Ekiert, "Peculiarities of Post-Communist Politics: The Case of Poland," *Studies in Comparative Communism*, Vol. 25, No. 4, December 1992, p. 360. See also Winiecki, who argues that "the Polish transition is bordering on the verge of a costly failure" (p. 833).

19. See, for instance, Roberto Donnorummo, "Poland's Political and Economic Transition," *East European Quarterly*, Vol. 18, No. 2, June 1994, p. 259.

20. Jerzy Hausner, Bob Jessop, and Klaus Nielsen (eds.), *Strategic Choice and Path-Dependency in Post-Socialism* (Aldershot, England: Edward Elgar, 1995), p. 6.

21. This has been argued by a former Polish prime minister, Jan Krzysztof Bielecki, in Teresa Torańska, *My* (Warsaw: Oficyna Wydawnicza MOST, 1994), pp. 57–59.

22. Ibid.

23. Michael D. Kennedy and Pauline Gianoplus, "Entrepreneurs and Expertise: A Cultural Encounter in the Making of Post-Communist Capitalism in Poland," *East European Politics and Societies,* Vol. 8, No. 1, winter 1994, p. 90.

24. Aleksander Bocheński, *Rzecz o psychice narodu polskiego* (Warsaw: Państwowy Instytut Wydawniczy, 1971), p. 115.

25. Korbonski, p. 300.

26. Ibid.

27. Bronisław Geremek, "A Horizon of Hope and Fear," *Journal of Democracy,* Vol. 4, No. 3, 1993, p. 102.

28. According to Marcin Król, after the collapse of communism in Poland, "there was briefly talk about introducing markets via some kind of enlightened authoritarianism." See Marcin Król, "Poland's Longing for Paternalism," *Journal of Democracy*, Vol. 5, No. 1, January 1994, p. 94.

29. Paul Lewis, "Civil Society and the Development of Political Parties in East-Central Europe," *The Journal of Communist Studies*, Vol. 9, No. 4, December 1993, p. 18.

30. *Polityka*, 31 July 1993.

31. Paul G. Lewis, "Political Institutionalisation and Party Development in Post-Communist Poland," *Europe-Asia Studies*, Vol. 46, No. 5, 1994, p. 797.

32. Klaus Bachman, "Poland," in Hanspeter Neuhold, Peter Havlik, and Arnold Suppan (eds.), *Political and Economic Transformation in East Central Europe* (Boulder, CO: Westview Press, 1995), p. 51.

33. Adam Michnik and Vaclav Havel, "Justice or Revenge?" *Journal of Democracy*, Vol. 4, No. 1, January 1993, p. 21.

34. Adam Michnik, "Testament of Lies," *Index on Censorship*, Vol. 25, No. 5, September-October 1996, p. 147.

35. Ibid., p. 147.

36. Barbel Bohley, quoted in *The New York Times,* 15 October 1996.

37. Michnik and Havel, p. 22.

38. Ibid., p. 25.

39. Ibid., p. 26.

40. Clarke and Wildavsky, pp. 330, 334, and 335.

41. Andrzej Kojder, "Corruption in Poland Today," *Polish Sociological Bulletin,* Nos. 3–4 (99/100), 1992, p. 335.

42. Ibid., p. 334.

43. *Przeglad Tygodniowy*, 18 September 1996.

44. *The New York Times*, 12 December 1996.

45. Joel Hellman, "Constitutions and Economic Reform in the Postcommunist Transitions," *East European Constitutional Review*, Vol. 5, No. 1, winter 1996, p. 56.

46. Ibid.

47. Mark Kramer, "Polish Workers and the Post-Communist Transition, 1989–93," *Europe-Asia Studies*, Vol. 47, No. 4, 1995, pp. 701–3.

48. Mitchell Orenstein, "The Failures of Neo-Liberal Social Policy in Central Europe," *Transition*, Vol. 2, No. 13, 28 June 1996, p. 22.

49. Carol Graham, "The Politics of Safety Nets," *Journal of Democracy*, Vol. 6, No. 2, April 1995, p. 143.

50. Poland spends 15 percent of its GDP on disability and old-age pensions—much more than is spent in any other East European country or elsewhere. Next to Poland is Hungary with 10 percent, and among OECD members the average is about 9 percent. Witold M. Orlowski, "Kulejacy tygrys," *Gazeta Bankowa*, 1 September 1996, p. 18.

51. Donald L. Horowitz, "Democracy in Divided Societies", *Journal of Democracy*, Vol. 4, No. 4, October 1993, p. 28.

52. Orlowski, p. 18.

53. *Polityka*, 5 October 1996.

54. Tadeusz Kowalik, "On the Transformation of Post-Communist Societies: The Inefficiency of Primitive Capital Accumulation," *International Political Science Review*, Vol. 17, No. 3, July 1996, p. 295.

55. Witold Trzeciakowski, "Transition in Poland," in Christopher T. Saunders (ed.), *Eastern Europe in Crisis and the Way Out* (London: Macmillan, 1995), p. 422.

56. Tadeusz Kowalik, "The Free Market or a Social Contract as Bases for Systemic Transformation," in Jerzy Hausner, Bob Jessop, and Klaus Nielsen (eds.), *Strategic Choice and Path-Dependency in Post-Socialism* (Aldershot, England: Edward Elgar, 1995), p. 138.

57. Dennis A. Rondinelli and Jay Yurkiewicz, "Privatization and Economic Restructuring in Poland: An Assessment of Transition Policies," *American Journal of Economics and Sociology*, Vol. 55, No. 2, April 1996, p. 156.

58. Kowalik, "The Free Market," p. 138.

59. Pond, p. 4.

60. "Prywatyzacja. Z Józefem Kowalczykiem, wiceministrem przekształceń własnościowych rozmawia Małgorzata Pokojska," *Życie Gospodarcze*, 30 August 1996, p. 29.

61. Ibid.

62. Kazimierz Z. Poznanski, "Political Economy of Privatization in Eastern Europe," in Hausner et al. (eds.), p. 216.

63. Quoted by Hausner et al. (eds.), p. 26.

64. *The Warsaw Voice*, 8 September 1996, p. 19.

65. *Gazeta Bankowa*, 18 August 1996.

66. Ibid. and *Polityka*, 10 August 1996.

67. *Gazeta Bankowa*, 18 August 1966.

68. Tadeusz Chrościcki, "Przebieg Procesów Społeczno-Gospodarczych w Latach 1990–95. Próba Oceny," in *Transformacje polskiej gospodarki w latach 1990–1995* (Warsaw: Instytut Rozwoju i Studiów Strategicznych, 1996), p. 44.

69. Alina Darbellay, "Farmers and Entrepreneurs in Poland and the Czech Republic," *Transition*, Vol. 2, No. 15, 26 July 1996, p. 17.

70. Stanisław Upława, "Głowne Problemy Transformacji Polskiej Gospodarki. Co wynika z badan IRiSS?" in *Transformacje polskiej gospodarki*, ibid, p. 94.

71. *The Warsaw Voice*, 22 September 1996.

72. *Gazeta Wyborcza*, 7 August 1996, and Radio Free Europe/Radio Liberty Newsline, 3 Feb. 1998.

73. *Poland: Country Report*, 2nd quarter 1996 (London: Economist Intelligence Unit, 1996), and Radio Free Europe/Radio Liberty Newsline, 3 November 1997.

74. Stefan Markowski and Sharon Jackson, "The Attractiveness of Poland to Direct Foreign Investors," *Communist Economies and Economic Transformation*, Vol. 6, No. 4, 1994, p. 527.

75. *Wprost*, 1 September 1996, and Radio Free Europe/Radio Liberty Newsline, 3 November 1997.

76. *Wprost*, 25 August 1996.

77. Chrościcki, p. 46.

78. *Poland: 1995–96* (London: Economist Intelligence Unit 1996), p. 22, and Radio Free Europe/Radio Liberty Newsline, 3 February 1998.

79. Estonia was ranked 23, Hungary 64, Latvia 67, Slovakia 75, and Lithuania 78. Quoted by *Gazeta Wyborcza*, 19 December 1996.

80. It was 98.6 percent of the 1989 GDP according to *Polityka*, 12 October 1996.

81. Chrościcki, p. 47, *Donosy*, 16 January 1998.

82. Previously it occurred in 1923–24. The other country that had experienced hyperinflation before is Hungary, where it happened in 1923–24 and 1945–46. Besides Poland two countries, Yugoslavia and the former Soviet Union, also experienced hyperinflation twice. All these countries are former communist states. Sachs, p. 40.

83. Simon Johnson, "Private Business in Eastern Europe," in Olivier Jean Blanchard, Kenneth A. Froot, and Jeffrey D. Sachs (eds.), *The Transition in Eastern Europe*, Vol. 2 (Chicago: University of Chicago Press, 1994), p. 286.

84. Korbonski, p. 300.

5 Czech Republic: Czechs Are Different

Amid all East European states the Czech Republic is, it seems, the least understood and the most underappreciated. There are two reasons for this. First, the Czech Republic has not been perceived by the West as a part of Eastern European that fell under Soviet domination in the aftermath of World War II, as a part of Germany did. Second, its past tradition of democracy and developed capitalism has been somehow forgotten, especially after the Warsaw Pact armies' invasion of Czechoslovakia in August 1968 and the imposition by Moscow of a hard-line communist regime.

Since then until the collapse of communism in Czechoslovakia in late 1989, it enjoyed less sympathy in the West than did Poland, where was born the first national independent trade union in the communist world, Solidarity; or than did Hungary, where were introduced, according to Western mass media, the first meaningful economic reforms in the Soviet bloc aimed at establishing market mechanisms. Due to these misperceptions the Czech Republic, which was created in January 1993 after Czechoslovakia's split into two states, is frequently seen by outside observers as being more or less on a par with other postcommunist countries of the region as far as its prospects for a sustainable liberal democracy and a viable market economy are concerned. Instead, the tacit assumption is that because the country was under communist rule for over forty years, like any other Eastern European

state, its chances of establishing an enduring democracy and a well-functioning market economy are similar to those of some of its neighbors—Poland, Hungary, and Slovakia in particular.

The other unspoken assumption, which follows from the previous one,
is that the past matters only as far back as communist rule extends. To
examine political and economic conditions farther back, and this is the last
implicit assumption, is unnecessary because the distant past has little if any
relevance to today's problems and its foreseeable future.

A question arises here: How far back in time should one go while
discussing systemic change occurring presently in the country? Perhaps the
past should be disregarded altogether, since the starting position of all
countries in Eastern Europe in the race toward democracy and a market
economy is much the same? Is it not true that all of them experienced
communism for about two generations and for this reason have similar
prospects for establishing a long-lasting democracy and a market economy?

According to this view, what counts, above all, in terms of prospects for
the future is the country's current performance in tackling a new regime that
is being built today on the ruins of the old one. This is an egalitarian
approach to social issues that presupposes that all people are equal in
capabilities, whether considered individually or as a group, such as an entire
society, for instance.

Regardless of how accurate this idea of equality is in relation to individuals, it is patently not accurate in regard to societies. In the latter case what
is being examined are a certain society's capabilities developed by it as a
group over a relatively long period. In other words, it is an assessment of
the past experience of a given society with a view to its political and
economic performance today and in the foreseeable future. The assumption
underlying this reasoning is that for a society as a whole it is easier to return
to its former political and economic system, if there is a will, than to create
a new one, unexperienced hitherto. For instance, it will be more difficult
for Russia to obtain a sustainable liberal democracy and viable market
economy, as it has virtually never experienced them before, than for the
Czech Republic, which was a part of a democratic, capitalist state until the
forcible imposition of communism soon after the end of World War II.
Furthermore, in the case of Russia not only will it be more difficult to
achieve the same goals as those at the Czech Republic but, and this is highly
relevant to this discussion, its chances of attaining them are considerably
lower than those of the Czechs.

Presently, democracy and a market economy are highly praised and much
valued all over the world. Of course the spectacular collapse of communism,

at a time when democracy based upon market forces flourishes, is the main reason for the ascendancy of democracy. The overwhelming majority of Czechs exhibit a strong desire to attain a system such as in the contemporary West, and this desire by itself increases their chances of success to a large extent. But what does increase their chances, even more than anything else, is that they experienced a democracy in the not so distant past. Indeed, there are still people in the country, unlike in Russia, who remember life under a democratic regime. These persons bring with them not only memories of the past but the experience, the know-how, and certain habits so useful and necessary again today.

This is not, however, synonymous with saying that the Czechs' future is predetermined and that the ultimate outcome of the current systemic transformation is a foregone conclusion. It is not. The chances that the country will develop in that or another direction vary widely, depending obviously on the specific scenario one has in mind. It is the argument of this chapter that the Czech Republic's prospects to establish an enduring liberal democracy and a viable market economy in the foreseeable future are extremely good.

Soon after the abrupt collapse of communism in Czechoslovakia, the country's economy began to decline. As a result of the implementation of systemic change, the country went through a period of recession. The sharp drop in output experienced in 1991, however, was overcome several years later. The GDP increase in the Czech Republic was close to 5 percent in 1995, and this occurred across all main sectors of the national economy though it declined to just over 4 percent in 1996 and only 1.2 percent in 1997.[1] Unemployment, another important indicator of the state of the economy, was in April 1996 very low by any current standards, registering below 3 percent. However, it reached nearly 5 percent in September 1997. In comparison to other Eastern European states its inflation of 8.5 percent was low, also, in 1996. It rose to 10 percent in 1997.[2] By the end of 1995 over 80 percent of the economy was privatized, significantly more than in any other country in the region.[3] In that same year the Czech Republic had a GDP per capita of $8,000, which is about half the average in the European Union and one-third of that in the United States but considerably higher than in any other postcommunist state.[4] Last, but not least, since the fall of communism in Eastern Europe, the Czech Republic is now the only country there where the former communist party did not return to power by winning elections. In all other countries of the region the ex-communist parties either have not lost power in elections or were returned to office apparently because voters were so disappointed with the performance of center-right political parties that they decided to give a second chance to the politicians they despised not so long ago.

That poses a question: Why are the Czechs outperforming all or nearly all other East European countries in their efforts to establish a liberal democracy and a viable economic system based on private property, competition, and market forces? At the outset of systemic transformation the Poles claimed that they were ahead of other states on the way from dictatorship to multiparty rule and from a command economy to a market economy and capitalism. Several years later they ceased to insist on being the leader in this field, however. When it comes to an overall assessment of transformation of both economics and politics, neither Poland nor any other state of the region contends any more that it is doing better than the Czechs.

That the Czech economy was not in such poor shape as, for instance, the Polish or the Soviet economy at the beginning of fundamental change does not explain all. That answer poses another question: Why in the late 1980s did the Czech economy perform better than that of most other communist state, with the possible exception of East Germany? Out of the many possible replies two sound more plausible than the rest. Either the economic system in communist Czechoslovakia differed greatly from other economic systems in Eastern Europe, or the Czech precommunist economy differed significantly from all others in the region and its impact survived until communism's very end and afterward, too.

Even a superficial comparison of the Czech economy as it functioned under communist rule shows that it was a copy-cat of the Soviet model, a model that brought about an economic crisis in the Soviet Union toward the end of the 1980s. Unlike in Poland, Czech agriculture was almost totally nationalized. And unlike in Hungary, a meaningful reform of the national economy toward the introduction of market mechanisms did not take place. The only attempts to implement some elements of a market economy in 1968 were nipped in the bud when Warsaw Pact armies invaded the country and stopped all efforts to reform communism in any recognizable way. Yet several years after the collapse of communism in Eastern Europe, the Czech Republic economically outperformed both Hungary and Poland, albeit in 1997 it was in an economic plight. Also, political development in that country after 1989 demonstrates that democracy struck deeper roots there than in the other two countries.

This, in turn, indicates that Czechoslovakia's relatively good economic performance in the course of communism when compared to other states of the region and afterward, since the demise of communism, relates in some way to its national economy functioning before communism was introduced. Or is there another plausible explanation to this puzzle? If one agrees that old habits, including economic habits, die hard, then certainly they cannot be destroyed in their entirety in a period of two generations, or just over forty years. It follows that many of those habits survived the communist rule until its collapse and came to the surface now when circumstances are, once again, favorable to them. There is no doubt that it takes much more time to change a person's customs, habits, manners, and so on, than to change institutions, systems, and laws. This phenomenon may be described as the iron law of social life. To put it differently, change of habits lags behind institutional change. Is that bad in itself? There is no general answer to it. It depends on what one wants to achieve through institutional change. If, for example, one intends to introduce communism through institutional change alone, then obviously the survival of some habits from the preceding period is often an obstacle on the way to this goal. If, however, one wished to establish a market economy also through institutional change, then clearly the survival of many habits from an era predating communist rule is by all means beneficial.

To reiterate, as a result of historical circumstances the Czech Republic is nowadays in a much more advantageous position than others to establish a new, postcommunist order because in its case it means, generally speaking, a return to the status quo ante. Before World War II Czechoslovakia belonged to the developed countries of Europe; it was not far behind Austria in terms of GNP.[5] At that time it was numbered among the highly industrialized countries of Europe. The country belonged to the ten biggest manufacturers of industrial commodities and to the seven largest suppliers of arms, as well as to those European states most dependent on export.[6] In the Czech lands, now comprising the Czech Republic, the average per capita GDP exceeded that of Austria, falling short of it only in Slovakia, the latter being a backward country by Western standards.[7]

Also, in the Czech lands agriculture was one of the most intensive in Europe between the wars, with yields per hectare above that of the European average.[8] In 1938, it is estimated, the industrial sector accounted for 65 percent of the total value of Czech production. At the time of the outbreak of World War II, it was the only surviving democracy in Central and Southeast Europe. Unlike other states in the region, the Czech lands have a tradition of religious tolerance and liberalism.

Whereas slightly less than 60 percent of people remained dependent on agriculture in Poland and Hungary in 1930, the figure for Czechoslovakia was only 35 percent.[9] It was also more urbanized than its neighbors. The illiteracy rate, too, was smaller there than in other East European countries. Once again, the differences relate especially to the Czech lands. In addition, that part of Czechoslovakia had a large middle class and a citizenry with a tradition of autonomous, pluralistic group activity as well as some experience in limited self-government.[10]

In the interwar period Czechoslovakia had a stable, multiparty or coalition government with respect for democratic procedures. In public life its people demonstrated a high degree of willingness to compromise and pursue give-and-take policies. Other countries of the region between the two world wars were different; their economies were backward, the majority of their people lived in poverty, and in the realm of politics they preferred dictatorship to democracy.

These differences in both politics and economics did not originate in the aftermath of World War I. They can be traced much farther back in time. Already in the nineteenth century, when the country was under Austrian rule, there were diets in Bohemia and Moravia, and the Czech lands people had representatives in the state parliament in Vienna.[11] Universal male suffrage was introduced there in 1907 by the Austrian government and was followed by the emergence of mass political parties. Furthermore, before World War I a wide variety of voluntary, self-help, and charitable organizations were established.

The Czechs also have a long tradition of industrialists' associations. The first one, the Guild for the Encouragement of Industrial Activities, was founded as far back as 1833.[12] Little wonder that autonomous employers' and industrial associations have been formed again in Czechoslovakia since December 1989, that is, only several weeks after the collapse of communism. This demonstrates vividly the survival of a long-standing tradition. If it had not been for that, it is highly unlikely, though not impossible, that the Czechs would have been organized in such a short span of time. It is also interesting to note that briefly after the downfall of communism Czechoslovakia set up an industrial policy, of which a guiding principle has been to support small businesses and thereby the growth of the middle class whereas in Poland, a government minister asserted that to have no industrial policy is the best industrial policy.[13]

The above discussion demonstrates that the Czech legacy is distinctly different from that of other countries in Eastern Europe despite the fact that it, too, went through a period of communist rule lasting over forty years. While under communist reign Czechoslovakia experienced a relatively high economic growth in the 1950s, which turned out to be short-lived. By 1963 the Czechoslovak economy was on a decline.[14] Several years later the Czechoslovak Communist Party attempted to reform its poorly performing national economy by introducing radical changes that ran against Soviet dogmas. This, among other things, led to the Warsaw Pact military invasion resulting in the abolition of economic reforms as well as other reforms relating to freedom of expression and freedom of association.

A severe, even by East European standards, policy of oppression followed. Approximately half a million people were "purged" from the communist party after the August 1968 invasion. Many persons lost their jobs as well. Perhaps to pacify the people even more and to recompense them somehow for the short-lived liberty, the standard of living of many Czechs and Slovaks increased after the invasion.[15] That may also account for a relatively weak political dissent afterward, in the last two decades prior to the downfall of communism in comparison to, say, Poland, where dissent was strong and widespread between 1976 and 1989.

Not until January 1977 was a dissident group, called Charter 77, set up. Within ten years following its establishment about 2,500 people signed the charter, among them Vaclav Havel, one of its founding fathers and a future president of Czechoslovakia and of the Czech Republic. Twelve years later, in November 1989, Charter 77 activists played pivotal roles in the Civic Forum, the organization that emerged to lead the "revolution," and in the coalition government that emerged in December 1989.[16] Unlike the Poles, the Czechs and Slovaks acted swiftly when opportunity arose to relinquish both communist rule and Soviet control. In less than a month they established a multiparty Government of National Understanding comprising communists as well as former political dissidents. The first free elections were held six months later, in June 1990, whereas in Poland it took two years before free elections were held.[17] But before that, in December 1989, Vaclav Havel was already elected as president of Czechoslovakia. In the space of twenty-three days the people of Czechoslovakia accomplished what in neighboring states, including Hungary, took several years. The transfer of power happened peacefully, and therefore it was labeled by the Czechs and Slovaks the "Velvet Revolution."[18]

Once the communists lost power a rapid repluralization of Czechoslovakia's associational and political life occurred. In about three months, by February 1990, over sixty parties and organizations were registered. In June 1990 over twenty parties took part in the general election. The Civic Forum emerged as the dominant political party, scoring almost half the votes. The communists emerged as the second strongest party in the Czech lands, with 13 percent of the votes.[19] Approximately 96 percent of the electorate cast a vote. The future Czech prime minister, Vaclav Klaus, was elected chairperson of the Civic Forum in October 1991. In that same year, the Civic Forum split into the Civic Movement and the Civic Democratic Party headed by Vaclav Klaus. His party turned out to be right of the political center liberal party, unequivocally in favor of a market economy based on private property. A program for economic transformation was adopted in Czechoslovakia even prior to the first free elections. It advocated a rapid and fundamental transformation, once again proving that when it comes to swift decision making and political actions Czechoslovakia was ahead of everybody else in Eastern Europe.

Two years later, in the June 1992 elections, Klaus' party in coalition with the small Christian Democratic Party won nearly 30 percent of the votes for the Czech National Council. Right-of-center parties won over half the seats in parliament.[20] To argue, therefore, that it was above all "the legacy of the communist rule that left a strong effect on the early stages of party formation"[21] and their activities is clearly wrong. To the contrary, it was the precommunist era legacy that had a strong impact on politics immediately after 1989, a kind of an invisible hand guiding the postcommunist politicians and their electorate toward new goals. Only with the passage of time will this impact become weaker as the nascent democratic institutions and market forces gradually supersede certain old habits and modes of activity.

By the mid-1990s, it has been noted by some observers that the Czechs more than other East European nations are keen protagonists of comprehensive, fast systemic change despite its obvious painful costs. One Czech posed a pertinent question: "Why is it," he asked, "that the Czechs continue to show such strong political support for a rapid transition, including virtually complete privatization, and tolerating wage controls?"[22] The reasons for it he attributed to economic factors and to features of the Czech national character. In his view it is the relatively low rate of unemployment and a distribution of shares to the population at large of the privatized property that gives Czechs a stake in seeing the transformation succeed. The exceptional patience and cooperation of the Czechs is the other reason. This answer, it appears, is only partly correct.

Several other East European countries also privatized through distribution of state-owned property, and yet people in those countries are less enthusiastic about systemic change than are the Czechs. Do these people not also have a stake in seeing the transformation succeed? Furthermore, unlike the Poles, the Czechs did not initially avoid a period of protracted decline in economic performance; nonetheless their government maintains by and large stability and popular support, which again is not the case in Poland. Why, then, are the Czechs patient in a situation where others are not? Certainly, it is not patience for patience's sake. There must be other causes for the Czechs' patience, and they lie in the realm of politics.

Unlike many other East Europeans, the Czechs, or at least a meaningful part of Czech society, understand the effect the economy has on political life. They realize that modern democracy is in practice impossible without capitalism, that is, without widespread private property and economic relations based on the principle of competition. Many Czechs argue that "to achieve freedom we must have a free market, the precondition of which is private ownership."[23] To put it differently, when most of the property is state-owned, the state is too powerful not only economically but also politically for a society of free individuals to emerge, and without it democracy cannot be established. This is the crucial point missed, it seems, by nearly all East Europeans with the exception of the Czechs. They see it more clearly than others not because they suffered more—the Russians undoubtedly suffered more over a much longer time—but because their democratic past made them aware that without economic freedom there is no freedom at all and hence there is no democracy which is grounded on it. Where there is one owner only, namely, the state, democracy is beyond reach; whereas when ownership is widely dispersed, democracy becomes a possibility.

In January 1990, just after the first postcommunist government was formed, most Czechs favored a market economy based on private property; only a small minority of about 9 percent opposed introduction of a market economy.[24] Various economic changes were discussed at that time, including a mixed economy, that is, one based on both privately owned firms and state-owned firms, with the latter still playing a meaningful role. Yet the Czechs decided not to introduce an economic system somewhere between communism and capitalism in terms of ownership, fearing it would lead them to neither prosperity nor democracy. As Vaclav Klaus put it:

> The task is to create a normally functioning market economy and a normally functioning political system based on standard political parties. We have no wish to undertake new social experiments. We have had enough of such experiments in the past. We want to play by the traditional rules; we want to accept traditional values. We are not interested in "third ways," the third way is the fastest way toward the Third World.[25]

The Klaus government's program for economic transformation adopted as its policy rapid change through liberalization of prices, internal convertibility of the Czechoslovak currency, and privatization. Klaus strongly contended that only a market economy "in spite of all its short-comings" is the best arrangement of economic relations.[26] Implicit in his argument was that competition is fair and just, as "only market relations will show who really deserves what."[27] For an economy to flourish it ought to be based on free, unrestricted competition; hence it must be a "market economy without adjectives."[28] In his opinion a social market economy attempts to combine two irreconcilable concepts and is impossible to realize, and for that reason he rejected it.

With regard to the pace and sequencing of economic change, which aroused so much heated dispute all over Eastern Europe, Klaus, from the beginning of economic transformation, argued that it must be done swiftly and without a preconceived order or step-by-step arrangement. Instead, he proposed "the introduction of as many changes as possible, as quickly as possible,"[29] without worrying unduly about sequencing. That means that he also opted for a comprehensive transformation.

Although Klaus was for swift change, he was aware that it could not be accomplished overnight; such change paradoxically requires a relatively long time to attain, and therefore people should not expect instant results. Unlike most other East European politicians, Klaus did not promise a land of plenty one day after the revolution; to the contrary, he warned Czechs that it would take some time before they would see the first palpable results of the systemic change. "We have learned," he said, "how to destroy, we have learned how to build, and now we must learn how to wait."[30]

It can be argued that a key element for success in fundamental transformation is time, a factor of which the Czechs are well aware. Their awarenesss, in turn, increases their chances of achieving success. More specifically, sufficient time is required for the systemic change to produce results, and it is the task of a prudent political leader to inform the people of this factor instead of raising their expectation unduly and thereby perhaps not only cutting short his or her stay in office but also destroying the process of systemic transformation.

What further enhances the chances of success in the course of radical change and uncertainty is the practice of basing one's policies on what will gain wide support or consensus politics. That implies not that politicians should follow the electorate's opinions but rather they should somehow guide the populace to an understanding of their ideas and policies. This requires certain skills in public relations and communication, skills in short supply in most parts of Eastern Europe, where the undemocratic past deemed them unnecessary and, therefore, provided politicians with little opportunity to practice them before 1989. Czech politicians, unlike, say, Polish politicians, were conscious of their shortcomings in this area. It was again Klaus who emphasized the importance of "creating a political and social consensus supporting the reform measures in [his] country."[31] That his party was reelected several times and has run the country in coalition from the downfall of communism to December 1997 indicates that the Klaus government maintained stability and popular support relatively long by keeping the expectations low and by applying government policies judiciously.[32]

These judicious policies have led to the Czech Republic's relative economic success, which in turn has contributed further to political stability. The Klaus government resignation in late 1997 does not distort that picture significantly. The high level of political stability, at the same time, allowed the government to implement less popular economic policies deemed necessary to complete the move from a command economy to a market economy—a feat the Czechs achieved by the mid-1990s. They progressed so far in economic transformation that they passed, it seems, a point of no return, which is not the case in several other East European countries.

Even the January 1993 split of Czechoslovakia into two independent states, the Czech Republic and Slovakia, did not negatively affect the process of fundamental change, as some political analysts expected. To the contrary, the split enhanced chances of obtaining a firm, liberal, democratic state and a viable market economy, since it is the Czech lands, and not Slovakia, that have a long tradition of democratic rule and a modern, industrial economy. Thus an argument can be made that the loss of Slovakia was a blessing in disguise for the Czechs because now they do not have to support economically the more backward part of the former Czechoslovakia, where standards of living were lower than in the rest of the country. Whereas the unification of East Germany and West Germany brought about a lowering of the standard of living in the latter, the split of Czechoslovakia brought about an increase in the Czech standard of living. More important, the Czechs know it so the split can be viewed as a positive factor in the Czechs' efforts to consolidate democracy grounded on market forces.

That the split occurred peacefully, unlike elsewhere in Eastern Europe, shows that the Czechs possess certain skills, experience, and habits often unencountered in the region. This is not to argue, however, that the Czechs are wiser than their neighbors or that this wisdom is genetically inherited, being passed from one generation to another; it is only to point out that past developments have enabled Czechs to learn not only how to achieve the desired goals but also how to achieve them at low cost. In that sense the Czechs can be compared to the post–World War II West Germans, who largely as a result of their defeat in two world wars also learned to be winners and not losers, to win in a bloodless way, and to keep the costs down. This process of acquiring new habits is gradual, hardly to be gained through formal education, and comes chiefly from learning by doing.[33]

For the Czechs the split of Czechoslovakia has not only economic advantages but political ones as well. Empirical evidence reveals that it is much easier to establish an enduring democracy in a country devoid of an ethnic minority. Slovakia, Bulgaria, Romania, Russia, and the former Yugoslavia, who have large ethnic minorities, are a case in point. Poland had large ethnic minorities between the wars and failed to establish a democracy then; but now having no meaningful ethnic minorities, the country has made more progress toward democracy than those countries having large ethnic groups. For the Czechs the split conveniently removed two minorities, the Hungarians as well as the Slovaks, thus eliminating a potential source of conflict.

Ethnic conflict has brought about authoritarian trends in many countries; therefore, it is frequently contended that a direct relationship exists between ethnic conflict and the failure to develop democracy. Furthermore, it is maintained, ethnic conflict makes the practice of democracy difficult.[34] Because today the Czech Republic is devoid of significant minorities, it can concentrate its efforts on other matters related to systemic transformation. That ethnic impediment, if it ever existed, disappeared together with Czechoslovakia; both of them belong to the past.

Although to create a sustainable democracy in a multiethnic society is difficult, doing so is nonetheless possible, as the Swiss example shows. Whether attaining an enduring democracy in a postcommunist society is possible without going through a process of lustration or screening of former communists remains debatable, however. Lustration, also known as decommunization, is the process of screening individuals elected to parliament or holding top political positions, determining thereby whether they once had ties to the former political police.

Immediately after the collapse of communism in Eastern Europe two opposing views emerged with respect to lustration. Opponents of screening argue that if implemented, it will create an additional hurdle toward democracy building. Why? Because it will alienate some individuals from democracy, in particular people who are still influential and who might, therefore, derail or slow down the process of establishing democracy. Thus their past activity should be ignored. If such individuals now support democracy and wish to be involved in politics, they should be given a chance. This was official policy in Poland until 1997 and remains the policy at large elsewhere since the downfall of communism.

Supporters of screening maintain that without it "there will be no transformation."[35] In their opinion, "Lustration gives democracy a breathing space, a kind of grace period during which it can put down roots."[36] It excludes from government its enemies. Fundamental change in society, so the argument goes, requires replacement of its elites. Those who say that it is best to forget about the past altogether and start afresh are not drawing the right lesson from the "dearly purchased experience of the communist era."[37]

Hitherto gained experience demonstrates that the no-screening policy may result in a government crisis. As a matter of fact, it led the Polish prime minister, Józef Oleksy, to resign after he was accused of being a Soviet and Russian political police informer. This accusation did not stop him from being elected a leader of the ruling ex-communist party after his resignation. That occurrence deeply divided Polish society and brought about much anger and cynicism among ordinary citizens, making some of them perceive politics as a "dirty game."

In the postcommunist world only the Czechs solved the problem differently. Informally, lustration had already appeared in Czechoslovakia before the first free election in June 1990. Cautious of potential political scandals, all competing political parties screened their own candidates, even if their names did not appear in political police files.[38] Later the Czechs passed a bill in parliament excluding, for several years, former political police and their collaborators from holding certain high political positions. By doing so they not only avoided a scandal like that in neighboring Poland but, more important, also passed an unambiguous message to the people that in postcommunist politics public *moral* leadership is a necessary condition, unlike before, under the Marxist-Leninist regime. Through the introduction of high moral standards in politics, in sharp contrast to what has occurred in other Eastern European countries, they gained credibility to a degree unparalleled by their counterparts elsewhere in the region.

Closely associated with morality in politics is justice. Communist rule brought about economic inefficiency and poverty as well as individual immorality. Therefore, it is sometimes contended, the downfall of communism is mainly a moral downfall.[39] Moral behavior is not prompted by capitalism as such, whereas personal immorality is an intrinsic value of the communist economy—a part and parcel of it. According to this view, an economy organized on communist principles is inefficient because it is immoral.[40] The moral failure of communism resulted in its economic bankruptcy. To achieve efficiency, morality must prevail. Capitalism grounded on market forces is efficient, so the reasoning goes, because of morality, among other things. In a nutshell, "Efficiency is part of morality."[41]

To ensure morality, rule of law must be established. The notion of the rule of law is based on justice; there cannot be the rule of law when justice is missing. Communism as practised denoted dictatorial rule, and this by definition excluded the rule of law, thereby making it devoid of justice as well. The link between morality, rule of law, justice, and the economy has been understood by the Czechs at large, but not by other East European nations. For Vaclav Havel, the Czech Republic president, "To administer justice, is clearly justified and natural."[42] Is it justified for others? The first no-communist Polish prime minister, Tadeusz Mazowiecki, opposed justice, as did Adam Michnik, his compatriot and a renowned political dissident under communist rule. To Michnik justice means "revenge" with regard to screening. Havel strongly disagreed with him, arguing that ordinary people are not driven by revenge but by "justice."[43] Furthermore, Havel maintained that to accomplish the transition from communism to capitalism and democracy, justice must be put into operation, thus implying that to attain the goals without it will be impossible.

The Czechs' different perception of justice is coupled with their different understanding of the role played by political leaders. To Havel, for example, the politician as a public figure is a role model to his people; he sets an example of how to act in the public arena. If he, the president, failed to obey the law, then the people would disregard it also—already the case in some neighboring states.[44]

This comprehension of justice and the role played by the politicians stems from a different perception of the individual in public life. Elsewhere in Eastern Europe the individual counts nearly for nothing and the society for everything, owing, perhaps, to communist and precommunist tradition in particular. It follows that group or society interests have priority over individual interests. Only the Czechs, it appears, understand that when the individual's interests are ignored, society suffers too. This concept prompted the Czech prime minister, Vaclav Klaus, to argue that when one "looks at the world, one must first focus on the individual— and everything that the individual represents."[45]

If the high moral standards set by Czech leaders are not just rhetoric, one would expect the levels of corruption, demoralization, and even bureaucracy to be significantly lower in the Czech Republic in comparison to other postcommunist states. According to a Western expert on Eastern Europe, "The level of demoralization and bureaucracy and, therefore, corruption appears to vary significantly [in the region]. It is the lowest in the Czech Republic and relatively limited in other Central European countries but it flourished in the Balkans and in most former Soviet republics."[46]

To argue, then, that one cause of low unemployment in the Czech Republic is the "weakness" of trade unions there in comparison to Poland and Hungary is to misunderstand Czech political culture.[47] Whatever the causes of low unemployment in the Czech Republic, they are only remotely related, if at all, to a low level of activity or powerlessness of Czech trade unions. Low unemployment stems, rather, from the legitimacy and credibility of the Czech government. Furthermore, Czech trade unionists are aware, unlike their counterparts in the rest of the region, that sufficient time is needed for systemic change to be accomplished. Only afterward will it be possible to reap the harvest of their work. They realize that their desires cannot come to fruition overnight.

The posture taken by Czech trade unionists also reveals another important feature of their political culture: They have trust in their government and, moreover, support it. Otherwise they would not be so placid, since they have a long tradition of trade unionism, and now, as they can strike legally again, they would have resorted to industrial action if not for the reasons mentioned above. According to the Czechs themselves, "Czech Republic trade unions have identified themselves with the strategy of a fast transition to democratic capitalism."[48] Fast transition means a painful life at the outset, and this is certain. What is uncertain, however, is that there will be a better life in the not-so-distant future. This shows that the Czechs have hope that what their government is doing now will be successfully accomplished before long. To build hope and trust requires certain skills proved by palpable results, which apparently the Czech political elite has managed to possess to a degree unmatched by its counterparts in most parts of the former Soviet bloc.

Certainly, the Czechs could not have acquired the requisite skills in the course of communist rule; otherwise postcommunist political and economic life in the region would not differ so greatly between one country and another. It was observed, soon after the downfall of the Marxist-Leninist regimes, that "as in other countries in the region, Czech leaders and citizens have returned to their pre-communist past."[49] When one ponders this, it comes as no surprise. The choice was obvious and natural: either to continue with communist practice or to act in a different mode. To act differently than hitherto would in fact eliminate the choice seemingly available to them: they could only return to their precommunist tradition. As this tradition varies from country to country so varies today's postcommunist political and economic transformation among these states. It could not be otherwise at the beginning of the new era, at least until different skills and habits are gradually acquired. For that to occur, more time is needed, among other things.

Although the Czechoslovak national economy functioned better than Poland's or Hungary's at the time of the collapse of communism, its transformation, unlike that of the other two countries, from its start contended with virtually complete state ownership of the economy; only slightly over 1 percent of the labor force worked in the private sector.[50] Within a few years, however, between 1990 and 1995, the GDP produced by the private sector increased nearly twenty times rising from 4 percent to about 80 percent and quickly surpassing the other two states in this respect. Simultaneously, the Czechs managed to redirect drastically their foreign trade from East to West. In 1989 more than 60 percent of Czechoslovakia's total trade was with the East. It was reduced three times, to only 20 percent by 1993.[51]

At the outset of systemic change Vaclav Klaus' group had relatively quickly prepared a comprehensive blueprint for economic transformation that was started rather abruptly in January 1991. The core of the government's transformation program consisted of three basic policies: macroeconomic stabilization, price liberalization, and privatization of state-owned property. Privatization was implemented in three ways: through restitution of nationalized property to the original owners or their heirs, through direct sale, and through issuance of vouchers for shares of state-owed enterprises, shares distributed freely to the Czechoslovak population.[52]

It is occasionally claimed that the voucher method will result in economic inefficiency because most vouchers were bought by investment funds set up by banks, which are under state control. Whether this will happen remains to be seen. Yet there is little doubt that privatization through the voucher method has given the Czechs a stake in its ultimate success. Perhaps this is one reason why the population has shown willingness to undergo painful transformation. How else to explain why the country endured few strikes during its first five postcommunist years when real wages stood significantly below (18 percent) their 1989 level?[53]

In spite of the Czech Republic's initial economic success, direct foreign investment in the country was relatively small, smaller than in Hungary; at about $2 billion between January 1990 and December 1993, it indicated that foreign investors had less trust in the Czech economy than in the economies of the country's southern neighbors. Admittedly, with regard to investment, capital flows to places where returns are expected to be highest, all other things being equal. That more investors' money went to Hungary than to the Czech lands is further evidence of the West's misperception of the Czech Republic, especially of its political stability and economic prospects.

Whether the hitherto untested method of privatization through distribution of vouchers has prompted foreign investors to be cautious and not invest large funds is unclear. Although in the West most of the discussion of Czechoslovak privatization has been focused on privatization by vouchers, it must be stressed that the real success has been due to other methods: small privatization, restitution and sale to foreigners, together with the spontaneous growth of private enterprises, which comprise the genuine private sector. It is generally expected that the dominance of the private sector will increase the efficiency of production and provide a long-term growth incentive for enterprises.

In terms of total investment, including foreign and domestic, it is the latter that is much more important because it is overwhelmingly larger worldwide. For that reason, it is interesting to note that in the mid-1990s investment as a percentage of GDP was 30 percent in the Czech Republic, whereas in Hungary it was 21 percent and in Poland only 17 percent. In the poor European Union countries it was 23 percent. Domestic investment comes from savings: The more people save, the better as far as investment is concerned. Statistical data reveal that the Czechs have a slightly higher propensity to save than either the Poles, the Hungarians, or the poor European Union countries.[54]

Caution is needed with regard to official statistical data coming from Eastern Europe; it seems that the Czech statistics are usually more reliable than others. In Poland, for instance, instead of being privatized de facto, state-owned cooperatives were reclassified as private enterprises, unlike in Czechoslovakia, where the government planned to privatize cooperatives because they "represent a socialist element in society, and are considered dangerous element for its spiritual, moral, social and economic health."[55] In Russia agricultural cooperatives have as yet been neither privatized nor reclassified apparently because the government believes that unlike the Polish government it has nothing to hide nor does it consider them a "dangerous element," as does the Czech government.

The drastic differences in approach to statistics and privatization of cooperatives in these three East European states illustrates perhaps better than anything else their contemporary political culture, one still deeply submerged in its collectivist tradition, another caring more for its image than for reality, and the last concerned above all about effectiveness. To relinquish these traditional approaches based on old habits, even though they are counterproductive, will not be easy for the Poles and the Russians; but for the Czechs doing so is irrelevant, since their method of dealing with cooperatives is, from an economic point of view, the correct one.

That the Czechs clearly outperform the two other states economically is also well visible in the area of agriculture. Ninety-five percent of agricultural land was state-run in January 1991, but by 1994 only about 19 percent remained state-owned. The labor force in agriculture in 1995 was 42 percent below the 1990 level, representing a clear increase in labor productivity.[56] Increased productivity means that agricultural commodities are now produced cheaper than before. For producers this denotes higher profits. Also, consumers benefit because goods may be sold at lower prices, especially when the monopoly is broken and competition encouraged.

Indeed, by 1995 the framework for a competitive market-oriented agricultural sector had been established in the Czech Republic. The share of agriculture in total economic activity between 1989 and 1994 was halved to 3 percent of GDP. The good progress in the transformation of the agro-food sector has in turn contributed to the successful overall systemic change. Current Czech agricultural policy, with its commitment to creating and maintaining a market-oriented, low support agriculture, could well serve as a model for other East European countries, which thus far lag well behind the Czech Republic.[57]

The Czech Republic created large-scale successors to the former state and collective farms. The government used chiefly sale and lease as well as restitution to former owners as a method of privatization for nationalized agriculture.[58] In 1995 owners of small farms, up to 10 hectares, represented only 12 percent of total arable land there, whereas in Poland farms smaller than 5 hectares account for half of total land managed by private producers.[59]

By the end of 1993 privatization of state property in the food industry was nearly completed in the Czech Republic, with 95 percent privatized; whereas in Poland less than one-third, or 30 percent, had been privatized by mid-1994. As early as July 1993 more than 80 percent of state-owned farms had been leased and more than 100 had been privatized by the Czech government.[60] This example alone indicates clearly that the Czechs' approach to systemic change in agriculture is faster, more comprehensive, and ultimately more efficient than approaches taken in other countries in the region. It has been shown also that the same relates to other sectors of the national economy as well as to the area of politics.

Does this imply that the Czechs are the most pragmatic people among the nations of Eastern Europe? The answer depends on what one means by the term *Eastern Europe*. If it denotes a geographical region, plainly the Czechs progressed farther and more rapidly on the way to a sustainable liberal democracy and a market economy than did the remaining nations of the region; therefore, in that sense they Czechs are more pragmatic. If, however, the term *Eastern Europe* depicts a political entity, then the answer is less obvious. Before World War II the term denoted a backward area of the European continent, at its eastern end, of which Czechoslovakia was not a part.

In the wake of World War II, the term's meaning changed somewhat; it became a political phrase denoting the area of Europe that fell under communist rule, including part of Germany. Thus Finland, though geographically farther east than many former Soviet bloc states, has not been deemed an Eastern European country, whereas Czechoslovakia was despite being farther to the west. Should the Czech Republic be considered an Eastern European country after the fall of communism? Not considered a country within Eastern Europe before the outbreak of the last world war, it became one only in the war's aftermath. What is it now? How should it be classified?

To give a clear-cut answer is not an easy task, and in this particular case it seems not to be important. The country appears to have recovered swiftly from the communist experience. Its political leaders and citizens in general are presently more concerned about economic prosperity and democracy than about a label attached to their country. And so be it.

The point is that the Czechs are more efficient or more pragmatic than the rest of the nations of the region not as a result of some superior blueprint for systemic change but, rather, because of a better and thorough implementation of it. In turn their skill stems from their previous familiarity with the democratic method and with a competitive economy or market. Had it not been for the latter, they would not have obtained so much in such a short time. The Czech example demonstrates that fundamental transformation is usually an evolutionary process rather than an abrupt occurrence, despite many claims to the contrary.

Although the Czechs made more progress than others, it must be pointed out, they did not have to start from scratch in terms of skills or habits; instead they made a U-turn, figuratively speaking, to a not-so-distant and well-remembered past. This, above all, is what makes the difference between them and all other former communist countries with regard to establishing a firm, liberal democracy and a viable economic system based on market forces.

NOTES

1. *Country Report: Czech Republic*, 3rd quarter 1996 (London: Economist Intelligence Unit, 1996), p. 15, and Radio Free Europe/Radio Liberty Newsline, 26 January 1998.

2. Ibid, and Radio Free Europe/Radio Liberty Newsline, 12 January 1998.

3. Ibid. The figure of 80 percent was given by the privatization minister, Jiri Skalicky. According to the Czech Statistical Office, however, the figure was only 66 percent.

4. *The Economist*, October 26—November 1, 1996, p. 98.

5. Jan Adam, "Transformation to a Market Economy in the Former Czechoslovakia," *Europe-Asia Studies*, Vol. 45, No. 4, 1993, p. 618.

6. Alice Teichova, *The Czechoslovak Economy, 1918–1980* (London: Routledge, 1988), p. 21.

7. Karel Dyba and Jan Svejnar, Chapter 2 in Jan Svejnar (ed.), *The Czech Republic and Economic Transition in Eastern Europe* (San Diego: Academic Press, 1995), p. 22.

8. Teichova, p. 33.

9. Sharon L. Wolchik, *Czechoslovakia in Transition: Politics, Economics and Society* (London: Printer Publishers, 1991), p. 3.

10. Ibid., p. 4.

11. Ibid., p. 10.

12. Ludek Rychetnik, "Can the Czech Republic Develop a Negotiated Economy?" in Jerzy Hausner, Bob Jessop, and Klaus Nielsen (eds.), *Strategic Choice and Path-Dependency in Post-Socialism* (Aldershot, England: Edward Edgar, 1995), p. 239.

13. Ibid., p. 245.

14. Wolchik, p. 27.

15. Ibid., p. 37.

16. Ibid., p. 39.

17. Paul Lewis, Bill Lomax, and Gordon Wightman, "The Emergence of Multi-Party Systems in East-Central Europe: A Comparative Analysis," in Geoffrey Pridham and Tatu Vanhaven (eds.), *Democratization in Eastern Europe: Domestic and International Perspectives* (London: Routledge, 1994), p. 165.

18. Wolchik, p. 50.

19. Ibid., p. 51.

20. Lewis et al. (eds.), p. 172. They won 105 of the 200 seats in parliament.

21. Sharon Werning Rivera, "Historical Cleavages or Transition Mode? Influences on the Emerging Party Systems in Poland, Hungary and Czechoslovakia," *Party Politics*, Vol. 2, No. 2, April 1996, p. 195.

22. Jan Svenar, in Svenar (ed.), Chapter 1, p. 5.

23. Quoted by Ladislav Holy, *The Little Czech and the Great Czech Nation: National Identity and the Post-Communist Transformation of Society* (Cambridge: Cambridge University Press, 1996), p. 158.

24. Ibid., p. 150.

25. Vaclav Klaus, "Transition—An Insider's View," *Problems of Communism*, Vol. 41, No. 1–2, January-April 1992, p. 73.

26. Quoted by Holy, p. 151.

27. Ibid., pp. 162–63.

28. Quoted by Martin Myant, "Economic Reform and Political Evolution in Eastern Europe," *Journal of Communist Studies*, Vol. 8, No. 1, March 1992, p. 124.

29. Quoted by Louis Haddad, "On the Rational Sequencing of Enterprise Reform," *Journal of Communist Studies and Transitional Politics*, Vol. II, No. 1, March 1995, p. 92.

30. Quoted by Galina Starovoitova, "Weimar Russia?" *Journal of Democracy*, Vol. 4, No. 3, 1993, p. 109.

31. Klaus, p. 75.

32. Svenar (ed.), Chapter 1, p. 191.

33. Haddad, p. 93.

34. Donald L. Horowitz, "Democracy in Divided Societies," *Journal of Democracy*, Vol. 4, No. 4, October 1993, p. 28.

35. Vojtěch Cepl and Mark Gillis, "Making Amends after Communism," *Journal of Democracy*, Vol. 7, No. 4, October 1996, p. 119.

36. Ibid., p. 123.

37. Ibid., p. 124.

38. Jirina Siklova, "Lustration or the Czech Way of Screening," *East European Constitutional Review*, Vol. 5, No. 1, winter 1996, p. 57.

39. John Clark and Aaron Wildavsky, *The Moral Collapse of Communism: Poland as a Cautionary Tale* (San Francisco: ICS Press, 1990), p. 17.

40. Ibid., p. 344.

41. Ibid., p. 344.

42. Adam Michnik and Vaclav Havel, "Justice or Revenge?," *Journal of Democracy*, Vol. 4, No. 1, January 1993, p. 22.

43. Ibid., p. 27.

44. Vaclav Havel, Vaclav Klaus, and Petr Pithart, "Civil Society after Communism: Rival Visions," *Journal of Democracy*, Vol. 7, No. 1, January 1996, p. 21.

45. Ibid.

46. Anders Åslund, "Niektóre wnioski z pierwszych czterech lat transformacji," in Marek Dabrowski (ed.), *Polityka gospodarcza okresu transformacji* (Warsaw: PWN, 1995), p. 366.

47. Ibid., p. 372.

48. For instance, this is the opinion of Ludek Rychetnik, p. 250.

49. Wolchik, p. 55.

50. Dyba and Svejnar, p. 29.

51. Ibid., p. 42.

52. Pavel Mertlik, "Transformation of the Czech and Slovak Economies, 1990–92: Design, Problems, Costs," in Jerzy Hauzner, et al. (eds.), p. 225.

53. Dyba and Svejnar, p. 45.

54. In 1995, savings as a percentage of GDP was 21 percent in the Czech Republic, 19 percent in both Poland and Hungary, and 20 percent in the poor European Union countries. *The Economist*, 26 October–1 November 1996, p. 98.

55. Mertlik, p. 221.

56. *Czech Republic: Country Profile* (London: Economist Intelligence Unit, 1996), pp. 15–16.

57. *Review of Agricultural Policies: Czech Republic* (Paris: Organization for Economics Cooperation and Development 1995), p. 35.

58. Erik Mathijs and Jo Swinnen, "Agricultural Privatization and De-Collectivization in Central and Eastern Europe," *Transition*, Vol. 2, No. 5, 26 July 1996, p. 12.

59. Alina Darbellay, "Farmers and Entrepreneurs in Poland and the Czech Republic," *Transition*, Vol. 2, No. 15, 26 July 1996, p. 18.

60. Ibid., p. 19.

6 The West's Approach to Postcommunist Eastern Europe

Nobody seriously argues that foreign assistance is irrelevant to the systemic change Eastern Europe has been undergoing since the downfall of communism. Yet the Western world's attitudes and policies toward fundamental political and economic change in the region leave much to be desired. Western politicians appear to believe that a mixture of economic assistance and verbal encouragement for transformation is sufficient to guarantee the successful change of communist regimes into liberal democracies based on a market economy.

The assumption is difficult to understand. Consider the fact that economic assistance for the Third World states since the 1950s has produced poor results thus far, and consider also that much evidence shows that the transformation of a Third World state into a Westernized regime seems much easier to accomplish than the transition from communism to a liberal democracy. Third World economies are, to a considerable extent, market economies based on private ownership. Yet there has so far been little success in bringing about their transformation into modern, Westernized economies with high living standards and a comfortable degree of welfarism.

Why, then, should the East European states be more successful with their systemic change than most countries in Latin America, Asia, and Africa? Why are many commentators in the West optimistic when they talk about transformation in Eastern Europe, yet pessimistic about the future of the Third World? Today this optimism seems to some East European observers to be sadly misplaced.

To illustrate: *The Economist* magazine argues that because "during the communist years, small groups of economists throughout Eastern Europe had always quietly studied Western economics under their desks," the success in transforming the command economy into a market one is almost certain.[1] This notion assumes that theoretical know-how possessed by a few persons is almost sufficient to cope with fundamental metamorphosis. Were this the case, by now the Third World would already have ceased to exist. Experience of a market economy, as opposed to theoretical familiarity with the concept, is not even mentioned as a factor in systemic change. Furthermore, political will and the ability to achieve desired goals is not even discussed.

It is often pointed out that to function efficiently, a modern market economy relies on institutions and rules established over literally centuries: property and contract laws and the courts to enforce them, accounting and bankruptcy rules, tax codes, pension and unemployment systems, labor laws, and the supervision of banks and financial markets. Until recently none of these has been present in Eastern Europe, let alone modern communication and transportation systems, which are practically nonexistent.

In addition, the game rules of the contemporary Western business community, domestic and international, are almost completely unknown to Eastern European politicians and their constituents. It is not that these principles were forgotten or abolished after the imposition of communism, but that they never really existed there, with the exception of the Czech lands. In other words, when the feudal system in the West gradually transformed into a liberal democracy and a market economy, a similar process did not occur in Eastern Europe. Hence, there is little there of relevance that can be drawn on.

The lack of previous experience of a market economy and of liberal democracy are the most serious obstacles to successful systemic change in Eastern Europe for the foreseeable future. This factor, however, appears to be only vaguely perceived in the West. To the contrary, it is thought that to introduce certain Western institutions, technologies, and capital into Eastern Europe is sufficient to guarantee success. However, the Third World practice demonstrates clearly that this step more often than not creates but a facade, behind which there is still a great deal of poverty and very little real democracy.

By now we know that technology is not culturally indifferent; that in terms of quality two products manufactured according to the same technology, say, in Germany and Russia, would be most unlikely to be of the same standard. And we know, well in advance, which of the two would be of lower quality and for what reasons.

Many people in the West seem to believe that poor people are poor only because of entrenched poverty from which there appears to be no escape, and that relief may come only from the outside, in the form of Western capital. To put it differently, what all of Eastern Europe lacks is capital to deal with the transition to a market economy and welfare state. The corollary is that credits, loans, and subsidies ought to be extended to Eastern Europe; this would be sufficient to guarantee success. What should be borne in mind, rather, are the enormous debts to the West owed by Third World and former communist states, if only to see that borrowed capital can be—and often is—squandered. Why should it be different now?

The answer supplied by the advocates of capital assistance is that occasionally in the past this type of aid did work, and they cite the examples of U.S. assistance to Western Europe and Japan in their efforts to rebuild their war-destroyed economies through large capital loans and credits. Although these are valid examples, they cannot automatically be assumed to apply to Eastern Europe. As far as Western Europe is concerned, economic assistance was extended to countries that had previously operated as modern market economies; the task was to rebuild them. In the case of Eastern Europe today, after the fall of communism, the situation is different altogether. The Czech Republic aside, the task envisaged is not to rebuild destroyed capitalism, a market economy, and liberal democracy but to establish them firmly for the first time, nearly from scratch. It is the argument of this chapter that the West's assistance to Eastern Europe since 1989 has not been as effective as it could have been had it known what the postcommunist states needed most to attain these goals.

When discussing Western aid to Eastern Europe today, the question arises, why should one bother about these countries at all? On what grounds should Western taxpayers support financially systemic change abroad, which plausibly should not be their concern? Is it a duty of the West to come to the rescue of the East? If not, then for what reasons ought aid to be given—for political, military, economic, or moral reasons or, perhaps, for a combination of these?

Furthermore, is it indeed in the interest of the West to see liberal democracy and a market economy flourishing in Eastern Europe? If not, should the West help the region anyway because charity is good in itself, and nobody disputes that? Opponents of aid to Eastern Europe contend, however, that charity begins at home and that it should therefore be earmarked for the unemployed or for job creation in one's own country, for instance, rather than transferred abroad.

With the collapse of communism, the downfall of the Soviet empire, and the breakup of the Soviet Union itself, the danger of another world war has disappeared. Accordingly the Soviet military threat to the West no longer exists. Unlike before, Moscow is now mainly preoccupied with its own domestic problems; its current efforts are concentrated not on external but on internal matters. Russia, the successor state of the Soviet Union, nowadays is economically in crisis and militarily severely weakened. Evidence of the latter is its troops' miserable performance in Chechnya, where Russian soldiers failed to defeat a seemingly poorly trained and equipped citizen force of a country inhabited by less than a million people. With the disintegration of the Soviet Union the security problem has gone as well, as the argument goes, and therefore now is an opportune moment to concentrate one's efforts on one's own country's problems—ecological, social, and economic problems in particular.

A reply often given to this argument is that though Moscow has been seriously weakened politically and economically in recent years, it nevertheless remains a nuclear power to be reckoned with. It is obviously better to deal with democratic Russia, economically prospering, than otherwise. Democratic countries, experience shows, are less willing to go to war than are nondemocratic countries, and who in the West wants a war? Therefore it is in the self-interest of the West to help Russia to establish a sustainable democracy.

But is that enough? Is assistance given to accomplish political transformation alone a sufficient condition to create a peaceful Russia, devoid henceforth of imperial ambitions? Perhaps an economic transformation aimed at establishing sustainable economic growth and development is an additional condition for Russia to become more like Germany and Japan in the aftermath of World War II, that is, a country in which aggressive behavior becomes a thing of the past.

Since the early 1990s two coup attempts took place in Russia; both failed. Is there going to be another one in the foreseeable future, or has the political situation in the country stabilized? When in May 1997 Russia's president, Boris Yeltsin, went personally to dismiss his defense minister, he ordered all army guards inside the Defense Ministry to be disarmed. Why has Yeltsin "every reason to be wary," six years after he replaced Mikhail

Gorbachev as Moscow's leader?[2] Is he not in full control of his military force?

If not, then it is probably in the interests of the West to provide him or, more generally, the democratic, liberal forces in Russia with financial assistance and thereby help stop nationalists and militarists from coming to power and enable peace to prevail. The fall of communism in Russia was followed by a drop in the standard of living there and led the country into an economic crisis. But, one may ask, what about the aid earmarked for other former communist states? Certainly they do not pose a military threat to the West. Why then, should aid be extended to them as well for no obvious reason? For instance, on a per capita basis, Albania was the top recipient of European Union financial assistance.[3] Admittedly, Albania, the poorest state in Europe with a population of a few million people, is by no means a threat to Western European security and stability. Most of the aid was squandered, anyway.

Furthermore, the Warsaw Pact, the Soviet-led military alliance in Eastern Europe, no longer exists. Why, then, should its former members receive financial assistance? Western supporters of aid claim that to attain an enduring democracy in the East is in the West's long-term interest. They argue that Russia, dispossessed of Ukraine, now an independent state, is clearly much less of a military threat than it used to be. Ukraine is a large, industrialized country with a population of more than 50 million people, and therefore without it Russia is drastically weakened militarily and economically. The West must therefore ensure that the Ukraine will never become a part of Russia again. For similar reasons, other East European states should also become a lasting part of the democratic world. Because their combined economic and military power is meaningful, they must never be allowed to fall under Moscow's domination again.

There is also an economic reason for extending aid to all former communist countries. If the assistance does not materialize, it is asserted, then the poor of Eastern Europe will cross borders to the West in large number, thereby creating a refugee problem at a time when unemployment among the European Union countries is high. A great influx of economic refugees would only exacerbate the problem, which in turn might have political repercussions. A consequence might be the strengthened position of nationalist, anti-immigrant parties a phenomenon already visible and steadily mounting. To avoid these problems, it is better to give the countries of Eastern Europe at least some financial assistance; this is viewed as a preemptive measure, less costly not only economically but also politically than the consequences of financial neglect.

Implicit in the ongoing discussion is the premise that the former communist countries will not be able to stand on their own feet economically, and thereby politically, without outside assistance. But is it really so? Opinions in this respect vary, especially in the West. Many Westerners wholeheartedly believe that without it Eastern Europe would fail in its efforts to attain an enduring democracy and a market economy with standards of living comparable to Western ones. For instance, it is strongly contended that "if Eastern Europe is indeed trying to return to Western Europe, an obvious implication is that success in the economic transformation will depend not only on the East, but quite fundamentally on the West as well."[4]

It follows that the West cannot escape "responsibility" for the systemic transformation currently taking place in the region. It is further claimed that in the absence of a generous and visionary approach by the West, achieving success in fundamental change will prove "impossible," "no matter how resolute Eastern Europe is with its own actions."[5] By success is meant the consolidation of democratic institutions and a well-functioning market economy. To this end, Western Europe should agree to free trade with the East not only in industrial commodities but also in agricultural ones and should open its borders to East Europeans "so that all of Europe can be a unified and integrated region." More specifically, economic success will be achieved when Eastern European living standards approach those of Western Europe in the next decade or two.[6]

That viewpoint, represented in the West by Jeffrey Sachs, U.S. economic expert on Eastern Europe, is based on an explicitly stated but false assumption that Eastern Europe was a part of the West, so now the problem it faces is only how to "return" to it. There is no doubt that usually it is easier "to return" to something than become a fragment of an entity one did not belong to before. And the latter is precisely the East European problem presently. That, in turn, implies its problem is not entirely economic in nature but political as well. There are not, however, clear-cut guidelines on how to cope with the problem. It is said that since the collapse of communism the situation in Eastern Europe is unprecedented, volatile, and unpredictable.

Writing several years after the "1989 revolution," Zbigniew Brzezinski, a former U.S. presidential national security adviser, argued that Western aid is most critical during the first stage of systemic change; perhaps it is even "essential."[7] Later on, access to Western markets and foreign investment becomes increasingly important. In his view, the inflow of foreign capital is not decisive after the crucial initial period of fundamental transformation. With regard to the inflow of foreign capital, he maintains that explicit preconditions and strict supervision of its utilization are necessary; otherwise "massive diversion of extensive theft of foreign aid is to be experienced."[8] Above all, the West ought to encourage the recipient states to develop some long-term mobilizing vision, one capable of sustaining domestic support for the required but painful transformation.

Almost a decade since the fall of the Berlin Wall the West has not come up with any concrete way to implement the long-term mobilizing vision it talks about. Does that mean it has no clue of how to create domestic support in the East for the much needed but painful fundamental change? Perhaps it is easier said than done. Were this not the case, then the East European states would have by now come up with an equivalent of the "American dream" suitable for their present conditions and traditions as well.

Immediately after the demise of communism, the richest countries of the West promised $45 billion to Eastern Europe over three years, between 1989 and 1991. By summer 1991 only 11 percent of the total commitment was disbursed.[9] This is not an impressive figure if one takes into account that the financial assistance given took place at a time when it was needed most. Western aid actually disbursed, including private investment, totalled $18 billion by the end of 1993. In fact, however, it was considerably less, since a huge capital outflow in the form of payments of interest and principles and of profits and capital withdrawals occurred at the same time. Therefore in reality one can talk about a net capital outflow from the region. To illustrate, it is calculated that a net capital outflow from Hungary, a country that gained the most investment from the West, reached $6 billion during that period.[10] It follows that foreign assistance was thus insufficient to sustain the desired result and could not play a determinant role in helping a smooth transformation.

Without doubt, involvement in multilateral organizations, along with Western economic aid and political support, provides a favorable external environment for the nascent democracies in the postcommunist states. Is this in itself enough, or should the West provide more positive incentives to firmly establish democracy in the region and to develop an even more extensive institutionalized framework for multilateral cooperation? Should it not also give more practical assistance to help liberal and democratic forces in the East and to impede the emergence of autarky and repressive and nationalist movements there?[11] It stands to reason that the benefits expected would outweigh the costs, since Europe as a whole would become a more stable, secure, and democratic continent.

Some political analysts go as far as to argue that a favorable or supportive international environment has been an "essential," perhaps even "crucial," explanation of the occurrence and the success or failure of democratic transformation in a given region.[12] Yet with regard to postcommunist states this important factor has been somewhat underrated. Between World War I and World War II the international climate was inimical to the stabilization of parliamentary governments in the region, which is not the case today. A lesson has been drawn from that experience, though assistance in material terms still lags behind verbal support.

It is frequently contended in the West that the main threat to liberal democracy in Eastern Europe is economic insecurity. Despite the current economic cooperation among the former Cold War enemies, the pain of marketization, made worse by the costs of demilitarization and European Union trade barriers, is generating popular support for the ex-communists and the extreme right.[13] Yet the West appears to be complacent about the overall situation in the region as evidenced by its limited commitment to the building of democracy in Eastern Europe. Its complacency seems to stem from the lack of a perceived threat: The Western alliance now feels secure because communism has collapsed, the Warsaw military pact is defunct, and the Soviet Union has broken up. This spells diminished interest in East-West relations by the late 1990s.

In addition, the West's preoccupation with problems of its own further weakens its interest in Eastern Europe's postcommunist transformation. Finally, helping to establish enduring democracy in the region is often a subordinate objective for Western politicians, for whom economic protectionism comes first and economic assistance to Eastern Europe is a vote loser. Thus short-term, palpable economic benefits overtake the long-term, less certain but more important political, military, and material benefits. As a consequence of the rather shortsighted approach to the difficulties experienced by the former communist states, integration of Eastern Europe with the European Union (EU) has thus far made very little progress. It has been observed that since 1989 the exclusiveness of the European Union is, if anything, strengthening.[14] It was only in 1998 that the EU started membership negotiations with five former communist countries: Hungary, the Czech Republic, Poland, Slovenia, and Estonia.

It is unfortunate that though the EU is able to support the emerging democracies to a much larger extent than it presently does, it is unwilling to do so for primarily political reasons. As is known from experience, policies to promote a market economy, democracy, and international integration are mutually reinforcing, and now is the time and the opportunity to extend such policies throughout the European continent. On a similar occasion, soon after World War II ended, the United States gave considerable financial assistance to Western European countries, helping them to restore democracy and to rebuild destroyed economies. The assistance given through the Marshall Plan was no less than 2 percent of the U.S. GDP over five years.[15] Today, however, the combined aid of the entire West is well below that level despite the fact that what is at stake now is, arguably, no less important than what was at stake then.

A move from stabilization to economic growth and development is politically imperative because Eastern Europeans are losing their enthusiasm and willingness to sacrifice, which they felt so strongly immediately after communism's collapse; their dismay is evidenced by the return to power through electoral victory of former communist parties in four East European countries. If the economic crisis in the region persists or deepens, there is an acute danger that social cohesion will be eroded and that nationalist tensions will mount. To avoid this, the West must open up its markets more to Eastern products; also caution with import liberalization and selective export promotion would be particularly appropriate in Eastern Europe.[16]

Less for economic purposes than for political purposes, foreign aid for the region can be used to cultivate more coherent and democratically organized political party systems, constitutions, judiciaries, and parliaments as well as other political institutions. This, in turn, should further help to establish legitimacy for the new postcommunist regimes and to achieve stability, which is required to complete successfully the process of systemic change. A law-governed economy, still largely missing, seems to be a precondition for a well functioning market economy in Eastern Europe. Without it is the prospect of a continuation of lawlessness and corruption, which would be unconducive to bringing about a prosperous national economy. This is an area wherein Western assistance can be meaningful, causing immediate and enduring effects.[17]

Foreign aid and capital flowing to Eastern Europe since 1989 stems from three basic sources: Western governments, international organizations, and private businesses and charitable institutions. Among the several international organizations that deal with financial assistance to countries in need, the most important are the International Monetary Fund and the World Bank. These organizations established in the aftermath of World War II to help rebuild the economies of countries destroyed by the war have no expertise in how to tackle East European problems of postcommunist transformation. That they believe otherwise is a bad omen. Yet this is not synonymous with contending that the roles of the International Monetary Fund and the World Bank have not been helpful and significant but only to say that the roles are much more modest than generally presumed.[18]

The postcommunist countries' two basic problems are political and economic, whereas the functions of the International Monetary Fund and the World Bank are almost entirely related to the economy. Half a century or so since they were set up, the two organizations have acquired considerable experience related to Western market economies devastated by war and to poorly performing economies of Third World countries, which, it must be stressed, are not command or communist economies. How to solve the postcommunist states' economic problems has been, it seems, no less difficult for Western economists than for their Eastern counterparts. The point is that neither the International Monetary Fund nor the World Bank has political experience and know-how of communism chiefly because there was hardly any contact between them and Eastern Europe before the downfall of communism. Yet to cope with economic issues of the postcommunist states also requires profound knowledge and experience of the region, since in real life the two are so closely intertwined that to separate them becomes impossible in most cases. Nowadays we live in a complex and interdependant world, where frequently economic decisions have political implications and vice versa.

What exacerbates the situation is that most postcommunist economies are simply too large and their transformation to capitalism too costly for foreign assistance to have more than a marginal impact. The West Germans have been transferring a large amount of capital, about 3 percent of their GDP, to the former East Germany. They are so generous to their fellow Germans in the east because East Germany unified with the Federal Republic of Germany. No wonder the West is not as generous to the rest of Eastern Europe, since nothing similar occurred there.[19]

To overcome the enormous cost involved in the transformation of communist countries into liberal democracies and market economies, which is beyond the resources of any individual state, assistance organized by a group of nations is a distinct possibility. In its own interests, the European Union, comprising fifteen Western democracies, most of them rich and adjoining Eastern Europe, should, one would think, extend a helping hand to the postcommunist states. Who will argue that it is not in the European Union's interests to see Eastern Europe politically stable, democratic, and economically flourishing? Nonetheless, its assistance to the former adversaries, though meaningful, is not impressive. It appears that neither the European Union nor the Western countries "have had a clear idea of how to assist the consolidation of democracy and they have been too protectionist and too ungenerous with their aid to stimulate the necessary dynamism in the new market economies."[20]

Since 1989 several institutions have been set up to deal specifically with postcommunist systemic change, among them Poland-Hungary Aid for Restructuring the Economy (PHARE), established by the European Union. The U.S. Agency for International Development (USAID) created a new entity—called the Bureau for Europe and the New Independent States—to manage aid to the new recipients in Eastern Europe. Unlike PHARE, it works primarily with nongovernmental organizations. Also established was an international bank, modeled on the World Bank, with the purpose of financially assisting Eastern European countries.[21] These institutions may turn out to be better suited than the International Monetary Fund and the World Bank to take a leading role with respect to fundamental change as a whole. Special circumstances, we know, require special institutions to address them.

Yet what is conspicuously missing among all the institutions established with the purpose of addressing Eastern European problems is an institution designed to deal specifically with issues not directly related to the economy. Instead, such an institution should be a broadly conceived international education organization created to address most aspects of public life deemed important in the course of systemic change. Its task should be to alter the traditional habits, beliefs, and activities that are inappropriate, ineffective, or counterproductive in attaining a sustainable democracy and a welfare state based on a market economy. Is it not strange that the American University is in Paris but there is none in Warsaw, where such a university is needed to expose East Europeans to Western ideas, especially in the fields of social and economic sciences, jurisprudence, and business and management, among others. Even though some parts of the region oppose establishing Western educational institutions, their resistance should be overcome with incentives. To continue to act in the old ways when circumstances have changed is a recipe for failure; therefore vested interests and inertia must be broken, and the sooner the better. With time these presently weakened vested interests will regain their strength, and when they do, to destroy them will be all but impossible.

Institutionalized assistance, organized to bring new skills and modes of activity to the region, is definitely much more important in the long run than financial aid. One cannot expect the influx of foreign capital to Eastern Europe to last forever. New habits, ideas, and expertise once acquired would exist indefinitely, however, superseding those that have kept Eastern Europe economically backward and politically unstable. In the long term, gains thus attained would be worth more than direct financial aid. Once the region prospers economically, financial assistance will be unnecessary. Furthermore, trade between Eastern Europe and the rest of the world will increase, resulting in an improved standard of living that will benefit all countries involved. This, in turn, enhances democracy's chances of being not a short-lived phenomenon but an enduring feature of Eastern European life.

The combination of an economically prospering region and a democratic Eastern Europe should lead to a reduction in arms and a cut in military expenditure, freeing monies to be spent on other purposes such as social security, education, health infrastructure, and transport and communication. Consequently, peace in Europe, having lasted already for over half a century, will be, most likely, prolonged for a much longer period.

The second kind of assistance, in the form of direct foreign investment, is badly needed at the outset of systemic change but becomes less important after a while. Initially, a demand for foreign capital, technology, new management skills, and marketing was high in Eastern Europe, but even then it was not crucial for domestic economic growth. Evidence shows that the Czech Republic, for instance, which in absolute figures received much less direct foreign investment than did Russia, progressed farther toward a market economy than did Russia, whose results hitherto are not very impressive.[22] In terms of investment, domestic savings are more important than an influx of foreign capital, as the example of the newly industrializing countries of Asia clearly demonstrates. In these countries over 85 percent of accumulation had to be saved domestically, so the implications for economic growth and development are manifestly straightforward.[23]

This is not to argue that the cumulative impact of foreign private investment, know-how, grants, and foreign debt relief linked to performance as well as assistance from international organizations such as the International Monetary Fund and the World Bank does not matter much.[24] To the contrary, that aid matters greatly if it is spent cost-effectively. The activities of U.S philanthropist George Soros seem to be a case in point. By 1993 he alone established foundations operating in twenty-three states with a total budget of $300 million.[25] In late 1997 he promised to spend over the next three years an additional $300 to 500 million in Russia alone. These foundations operate mainly in education, the arts, mass media, the sciences, and the humanities, filling an important gap in areas crucial to the overall successful completion of systemic change, but underappreciated and hence neglected by Western governments.

In relation to fundamental transformation, the most powerful single leverage the West has in its possession to ensure Eastern European countries head the way it wants is the European Union, which most, if not all, former communist states wish to join. Now comprising fifteen states, the European

Union is a political and economic institution of wealthy democratic countries. The East Europeans desire to join the European Union less for political reasons, which led to its formation, than for economic ones. They believe that European Union membership will almost overnight solve their economic problems inherited from the communist past. They also believe that membership will immediately bring about high standards of living for most of them, comparable to those in the West.

Whether this perception is realistic is not an issue here. What matters is that it gives the European Union enormous influence in Eastern Europe that it could and should utilize in a way beneficial to itself as well as to its Eastern neighbors. Thus far the European Union has played its cards rather poorly. Soon after the collapse of communism, it should have produced a timetable for all potential candidates with a detailed list of necessary and sufficient conditions required to become a member. The timetable for membership should not be a long-term one for two reasons. If membership were delayed, say, one generation or about twenty-five years, then it would lose much of its attraction because Eastern Europeans would not want to wait long to see tangible results. Under the old regime Eastern Europeans were told time and again that it would take many years to achieve economic prosperity. It never happened. They simply do not want to listen to the same story again.

One must also consider that an extended timetable may not bring about the expected results. Systemic transformation ought to be done rapidly; otherwise change may stop halfway as a result of the unavoidable pain it causes. There is no doubt that the long duration of fundamental change seriously affects the process itself; the shorter the time, the greater the chances of its ultimate success. Not only does a long transformation prolong suffering, anxiety, and feelings of insecurity in many individuals, it also reinforces the vested interests of persons and institutions profiting from the volatile situation and thus willing to defend it vigorously. It follows that the revolution must be completed swiftly, or it may fizzle out.

In respect to establishing a sustainable democracy and a prosperous market economy in Eastern Europe, whether one day countries of the region will join the European Union is less important than recognizing that now is the opportunity to induce them to do so. Once democracy and capitalism strike a deep root in Eastern Europe, whether the countries of the region are in or outside the European Union will become almost irrelevant because by then they will have reached a point of no return. Of course, European Union membership even then would be beneficial to them, in the domain of the economy in particular.

However, only in July 1997 did the European Commission officially recommend that five East European countries—the Czech Republic, Hungary, Poland, Estonia, and Slovenia—be invited for talks on the first wave of European Union eastward expansion. The European Union set three main criteria for beginning accession talks: (1) political, which meant stable institutions that guarantee democracy, the rule of law, human rights, and the protection of minorities; (2) economic, which meant a functioning market economy that can withstand competitive pressure from other European Union countries; and (3) the ability to take on the obligations of membership, in particular implementing the common law of the European Union. Of the ten Eastern European applicants only the aforementioned countries were regarded as capable of meeting the criteria in the midterm; Slovakia, Bulgaria, Romania, Lithuania, and Latvia were not.

But we do not live by bread alone even in times of economic hardship; security for many East Europeans is their next priority to be addressed since they regained independence. To secure lasting security most Eastern European states are eager to join NATO, the Western military institution comprising the United States, Canada, nearly all of Western Europe, and Turkey. Because the postcommunist countries of Eastern Europe perceive Moscow as a potentially serious threat to their recently regained independence despite the Soviet Union's breakup and the collapse of communism, several of them have already applied for NATO membership.

This, in turn, gives the West another excellent opportunity to ensure that the systemic change in the region continues to proceed as it desires. Although democratic rule has thus far not been a precondition to join NATO, it should be made so henceforth. Also, a national economy based on market principles and friendly relationships with their neighbors should be declared as the other necessary condition to enter it. Admittedly, this enhances the prospect of prevailing peace in Europe, and perhaps elsewhere, well beyond the twentieth century. It also gives enormous impetus to the nascent democracies and market economies to become fully fledged and long-lasting as well.

Initially, Russia was against the eastward expansion of NATO, fearing a stronger NATO would diminish its own security. After several years of protracted negotiations with NATO officials and Western heads of government, however, Moscow reluctantly agreed to the expansion of NATO into Eastern Europe under certain conditions. A deal was reached in Moscow in May 1997. Soon after a NATO-Russia Act was signed by the Russian president and his Western counterparts. The act includes a pledge by the alliance that it has no intention of permanently stationing substantial forces in the new member states; the Czech Republic, Hungary, and Poland are widely seen as the most likely countries to join NATO before the end of the twentieth century.[26]

In an effort to ease Russian concerns, NATO expressed no wish to start deploying divisions in Poland or to base nuclear missiles in the new member states.[27] It also formally acknowledged Russia's role in the management of European security. This is an important shift in the direction of making NATO not just a military alliance but a system of collective security. The NATO-Russia Act, signed in Paris, gives Moscow full consultation rights with the alliance through a NATO-Russia Council. The United States describes this as "a voice, not a veto," allowing for the maximum possible consultation and joint decision taking.[28]

Under the agreement, called the Founding Act on Mutual Relations, Cooperation and Security between NATO and the Russian Federation, Moscow will appoint an ambassador to NATO and will send liaison officers to several alliance command headquarters. NATO will also station liaison officers in Moscow and other central command centers. For its part, Moscow will also send civilian and military personnel to NATO headquarters in Brussels. In addition, a secretariat will be established to serve the new NATO-Russia Permanent Joint Council, the proposed forum for all consultations.[29] Although the deal would give the Russians a special status that status is not legally binding.

Immediately after Russia signed the agreement, it began to reap rewards from the NATO pact, with the Organization of Economic Cooperation and Development (OECD) offering Moscow a cooperation pact to help the country to liberalize its economy and strengthen its ties with the West. Ministers from the twenty-nine member states of the OECD, generally seen as the international association of developed free-market economies, signed a deal in Paris with the Russian foreign minister; they promised to help Moscow establish a "fully fledged market economy within a framework of democratic institutions."[30]

The deal underlines the political trade-off between Russia's acceptance of NATO expansion eastward and Western efforts to speed up Moscow's membership in international economic organizations. In early 1997 the U.S. president, Bill Clinton, promised that if Moscow signed a NATO-Russia agreement, he would propose full Russian membership in the Group of Seven, consisting of the seven richest states.

It appears that Russia has resented the relatively swift integration of its former East European satellites into Western bodies, whereas its own membership negotiations have been more protracted. The OECD, for instance, set up in the aftermath of World War II, already includes the Czech Republic, Hungary, and Poland—which will also be the first new NATO members—but not Russia; it has, however, accepted the principle of Russia's membership. Russia is also negotiating for membership of the World Trade Organization, where it has observer status. Its current prospects for joining look better than ever before.[31] Moscow is already a member of the International Monetary Fund and the World Bank.[32]

A few days after the NATO-Russia pact was signed, NATO also signed a security agreement with the Ukraine. The NATO-Ukraine accord is similar to an alliance reached with Russia and lays the ground work for closer cooperation in many military and political areas.[33]

Several weeks later NATO formally invited Hungary, Poland, and the Czech Republic to join on its fiftieth anniversary, in 1999. The NATO leaders reassured other former communist states, particularly Slovenia and Romania, that there will be further waves of enlargement in which they will stand a good chance of being brought into the Western security alliance. The invitation to join the organization has to win ratification from all sixteen NATO member parliaments.

It appears that the West's relations with Russia as regards security issues are better and have proceeded faster than the economic ones though it is the latter that still require more cooperation as well as Western aid and know-how. Suffice it to say that by the end of 1995 the Russian foreign debt reached $124 billion, thus overtaking Brazil as the most heavily indebted country in the world.[34] Merely servicing it requires $20 billion annually. For Russia, this proved to be impossible in practice; in 1994 it paid less than $1 billion of its debt.[35] What exacerbates Russia's economic plight even more is the flight of capital abroad: About $50 billion left Russia in 1994 alone, although some argue that the figure for 1994 "should be $80 billion," whereas foreign direct investment in the Russian economy during that same year was a mere $1.2 billion.[36]

Indeed, foreign direct investment in Russia is low by any measure; by the end of 1995 it reached some $5.5 billion, with approximately $1.9 billion invested in 1995.[37] This contrasts sharply with China, where $83 billion was invested between 1984 and 1994, and $41.7 in 1996 alone.[38] Per capita foreign investment in Russia is only $27—much lower than in most East European countries.[39] Russia draws little foreign capital because it lacks, among other things, political stability and lucid tax legislation, whereas crime and corruption are rampant.[40] Some political analysts go as far as to argue that "if conditions are not created to encourage foreign investment and entrepreneurship, then Russian economic reform efforts will fail."[41]

Also in the area of foreign trade, the West does not help Russia's economy to the extent it does for some Third World countries. Russian exports remain subject to many quotas and high tariffs.[42] Despite this, whereas in 1989 the Soviet Union conducted about one-fourth of its trade with the West, in 1993 more than three-fourths of Russian trade was with Western countries.[43] Undoubtedly a lack of economic freedom in Russia is an additional obstacle to stepping up trade with the West. Russia ranked 105th among 115 nations worldwide in terms of economic freedom in 1995 according to a study conducted by the Canadian Fraser Institute.[44]

In comparison to Russia, the influx of foreign direct investment to Poland was considerably higher. Between 1990 and 1994 it was, however, Hungary that attracted more investment than any other East European state. Out of the total $12 billion invested in the region in that period, half went to Hungary, about a quarter to the Czech Republic, and less than a sixth to Poland, the latter being the only other East European state to attract significant foreign capital. No other nation managed to bring in more than $400 million.[45] In per capita terms, direct foreign investment in Hungary was $558, in the Czech Republic $242, and in Poland a meager $28.[46] The inflow of foreign investment to Eastern Europe between 1990 and 1994 contrasts sharply with what went during the same period to developing countries. It comprised only 7 percent of the latter.[47]

There are several reasons why Poland has failed thus far to attract more direct foreign investment, which it greatly requires nowadays. The country has not yet developed the elite consensus for a really effective foreign investment policy; consequently it lacks a coherent policy to attract investment from abroad. It is also slow to establish the financial, legal, technological, and institutional infrastructure necessary to support foreign investment. In addition, since 1989 foreign investment in Poland has been obstructed by an array of bureaucratic barriers and murky regulations. Also, weak governments, often disunited, resulted in repeated policy reversals coupled with their inability to develop a clear and stable approach to direct foreign investment. They failed, too, to set up working consultative devices to mediate worker-employee relations. In short, administrative chaos, still prevailing in Poland, is a serious impediment to attracting more foreign investment. It was only in 1996 that Poland overtook Hungary as the country in the region with the largest foreign investment in absolute figuers ($20.6 billion from 1989 to the end of 1997).

Another hurdle to Poland's economic growth is its large foreign debt incurred in the course of communist rule. After the collapse of communism in the country Western creditors reduced it greatly, by about $20 billion, to an estimated $43.9 billion in 1995.[48] This, in turn, allowed Poland to resume servicing the debt in its entirety for the first time since the late 1970s.[49] Resumption of debt payment should enhance Poland's creditworthiness, resulting in increased foreign trade, which, as in Russia, has been redirected to the West, with Germany quickly becoming Poland's biggest trade partner.

With regard to the Czech Republic, the third country discussed here, shortly after the "Velvet Revolution" its government decided to use a minimum of foreign assistance and has even refrained from relations with the World Bank. As then Prime Minister Vaclav Klaus explained, "The role of external factors in this process [of systemic change] is relatively small."[50] His view is shared by a former chief foreign aid coordinator of Czechoslovakia who identified the prevalent mood in the country: He declared, "We don't want the money [from foreign aid institutions]."[51]

What makes the Czechs less eager to pursue foreign aid than other East European nations is their undoubted success in the implementation of fundamental transformation and their awareness that what counts more in terms of economic growth and development is reliance on one's own savings in connection with investment. The West's appraisal of the Czech Republic, in contradistinction to Russia, is high. In the words of a Western observer, "So successful have been the economic reforms since the 'velvet revolution'—spearheaded by President Vaclav Havel and Prime Minister Vaclav Klaus—that the USA has already announced 'graduation' for the Czech Republic by the close of 1996."[52]

To recapitulate, the foregoing discussion makes manifestly clear that although the West has at its disposal the means to ensure that the political and economic transformation of Eastern Europe moves in the direction desired by Western nations, it lacks the vision and, above all, the willingness to pursue these aims wholeheartedly. There are two reasons for this; one is the cost involved, and the other is an unawareness of what the East needs most today.

The sheer cost makes Western politicians apprehensive. If they increase financial aid much more, they fear, they may lose electoral support; and that factor, it seems, matters more to them than anything else. Owing to this, the West's future capital assistance to the region will probably not be considerably above the level reached by the late 1990s. Projected levels would be higher if Western leaders were to convince their people that increased aid is in their own best long-term interests. The politicians, however, are not prepared to take the chance. Once the military threat posed by Moscow and the likelihood of another world war diminished greatly, most Westerners and their politicians became complacent and hence less keen to spend large amounts of money on matters related to international security and issues of peace and war. Experience shows that only immediate and unmistakably clear military threats and the likelihood of war make people ready to spend much capital on security-related matters; otherwise we tend to minimize security issues. That posture is taken by democratic regimes in particular.

Furthermore, the West seems to believe that money alone can solve almost all problems involved with the ongoing fundamental change in Eastern Europe. This, however, is not the case. In the long run, not money, not even new institutions and laws, but human beings' habits, ideas, know-how, and modes of activity matter most. This fact has hitherto been little understood by the West, and therefore almost entirely overlooked, in the course of its dealings with Eastern Europe since communism crumpled.

NOTES

1. *The Economist*, 21 September, 1991.

2. *The Australian*, 26 May 1997.

3. *The Weekend Australian*, 15–16 March 1997.

4. This is the opinion of Jeffrey Sachs, *Poland's Jump to the Market Economy* (Cambridge, MA: MIT Press, 1993), p. 6.

5. Ibid.

6. Ibid.

7. Zbigniew Brzezinski, "The Stages of Postcommunist Transformation," in Yevhen Bystrycky et al. (ed.), *The Political Analysis of Postcommunism* (Kiev: Political Thought, 1995), p. 110.

8. Ibid., p. 12.

9. Ivan T. Berend, "Alternatives of Transformation: Choices and Determinants: East-Central Europe in the 1990s," in Beverly Crawford (ed.), *Markets, States and Democracy: The Political Economy of Postcommunist Transformation* (Boulder, CO: Westview Press, 1995), p. 142.

10. Ibid., p. 143.

11. Adrian G. V. Hyde-Price, "Democratization in Eastern Europe: The External Dimension," in Geoffrey Pridham and Tatu Vanhaneu (eds.), *Democratization in Eastern Europe: Domestic and International Perspectives* (London: Routledge, 1994), p. 146.

12. For instance, Geoffrey Pridham, "The International Dimension of Democratisation: Theory, Practice, and Inter-Regional Comparisons," in Geoffrey Pridham, Eric Herring, and George Sanford (eds.), *Building Democracy? The International Dimension of Democratisation in Eastern Europe* (London: Leicester University Press, 1994), p. 7.

13. Eric Herring, "International Security and Democratisation in Eastern Europe," in Pridham et al., p. 111.

14. Berend, p. 146.

15. Ralf Dahrendorf, *Reflections on the Revolution in Europe* (New York: Times Books, Random House, 1990), p. 163.

16. Friedrich Levcik, "Economic Transformation in the East: A Critical Appraisal of Its Development and Suggestions for a Possible Way Out," in Christopher T. Saunders (ed.), *Eastern Europe in Crisis and the Way Out* (London: Macmillan, 1995), p. 26.

17. Hans von Zon, "Alternative Scenarios for Central Europe," in Jerzy Hausner, Bob Jessop, and Klaus Nielsen (eds.), *Strategic Choice and Path-Dependency in Post-Socialism* (Aldershot, England: Edward Elgar, 1995), p. 117.

18. Stanisław Gomułka, "The IMF-supported Programs of Poland and Russia, 1990–1994: Principles, Errors, and Results," *Journal of Comparative Economics*, No. 20, 1995, p. 316.

19. Pinder, p. 319.

20. Ibid.

21. Janine Wedel, "U.S. Aid to Central and Eastern Europe: Results and Recommendations," *Problems of Post-Communism*, Vol. 42, No. 3, May-June 1995, p. 47.

22. László Csaba, *The Capitalist Revolution in Eastern Europe: A Contribution to the Economic Theory of Systemic Change* (Aldershot, England: Edward Elgar, 1995), p. 290.

23. Ibid.

24. Gomułka, p. 343.

25. Johnathan Sunley, "Post-Communism: An Infantile Disorder," *The National Interest*, No. 44, summer 1996, footnote 9 on p. 10, and Radio Free Europe/ Radio Liberty Newsline, 21 October 1997.

26. *The Australian*, 16 May 1997.

27. *The Australian*, 15 May 1997.

28. *The Australian*, 28 May 1997.

29. Ibid.

30. *The Australian*, 29 May 1997.

31. Ibid.

32. Iu Shishkov, "Russia's Thorny Path to the Global Economy," *Russian Social Science Review*, Vol. 3, No. 6, November-December, 1996, p. 13.

33. *The Weekend Australian*, 31 May–1 June 1997. See also *The Age*, 31 May 1997.

34. Stefan Hedlund and Niclas Sundström, "The Russian Economy after Systemic Change," *Europe-Asia Studies*, Vol. 48, No. 6, September 1996, p. 910.

35. Igor Mirman, "Gloomy Prospects for the Russian Economy," *Europe-Asia Studies*, Vol. 48, No. 5, July 1996, p. 747.

36. Hedlund and Sundström, p. 910.

37. Peter Rutland, "Russia's Unsteady Entry into the Global Economy," *Current History*, Vol. 95, No. 603, October 1996, p. 327.

38. Ibid., and *The Australian*, 26 May 1997.

39. Natalia Gurushina and Zsofia Szilagyi, "Seeking Foreign Investment in Hungary and Russia," *Transition*, Vol. 2, No. 2, 26 January 1996, p. 24.

40. Ibid., p. 22.

41. Marshall Goldman and Ethan B. Kapstein, "Economic Conversion in Perspective," *Demokratizatsyia*, Vol. 4, No. 1, winter 1996, p. 67.

42. Rutland, p. 323.

43. Susanne M. Birgerson and Roger E. Kanet, "East-Central Europe and the Russian Federation," *Problems of Post-Communism*, Vol. 42, No. 4, July-August 1995, p. 29.

44. As quoted in *The Australian*, 26 May 1996.

45. Anne Henderson, "The Politics of Foreign Investment in Eastern Europe: Lessons from the Polish and Hungarian Experiences," *Problems of Post-Communism*, Vol. 42, No. 3, May-June 1995, p. 53.

46. Ibid. According to another source, however, the figures differ significantly. Allegedly, direct foreign investment over the period 1990 to 1995 in Poland reached $7.9 billion and was second in the region only to Hungary which attracted $11 billion. In per-head terms it was $114 in Poland to the end of 1994; the country falls in fourth place after Hungary ($691), the Czech Republic ($300), and Estonia ($291). In 1995 direct foreign investment in Poland was estimated to be $2.5 billion. *Poland: Country Report*, 2nd quarter 1996 (London: Economist Intelligence Unit, 1996).

47. Henderson, p. 52.

48. Ibid.

49. Gomułka, p. 34; and *Country Profile: Poland*, 3rd quarter 1996 (London: Economist Intelligence Unit, 1996), p. 3.

50. Quoted in Wedel, p. 48.

51. Quoted in ibid.

52. Ernesto Hernàndez-Catà, "Russia and the IMF: The Political Economy of Macro-Stabilization," *Problems of Post-Communism*, Vol. 42, No. 3, May-June 1995, p. 28.

7   Conclusion: Eastern European Prospects for Liberal Democracy and a Market Economy

The outlook for a liberal democracy and a market economy is certain to vary from country to country in Eastern Europe. This comes as no surprise to anyone, since everybody concerned with the region's postcommunist systemic change expected inconsistency. As regards the countries examined in this book, prospects for a sustainable, enduring democracy and a prosperous economy functioning on market principles progress steadily as one moves from east to west; that is, they are brighter for Poland in comparison to Russia, and for the Czech Republic in comparison to Poland. This is to argue, however, not that the end results will definitely be different for each country but that the chances each country has of obtaining its goals are unequal.

With regard to the foreseeable future, one can talk about certain trends or tendencies that may continue for some time, but obviously not in perpetuity. Social life, unlike science, is not governed by laws or tenets that are always valid, just waiting to be discovered and utilized thereafter to attain some envisaged aims. The future will thus forever remain uncertain, like early weather forecasts. The likelihood that a weather forecast is correct goes up as our knowledge about the weather and its past patterns increases. A similar situation prevails in social life, including politics and economics.

Due to this, the past matters and usually has a great impact on the immediate future. It follows that the past can and should be used as an indicator of things to come in the foreseeable future. Yet it will always remain just that, an indicator with a degree of probability below 100. This, nevertheless, should not deter an individual from venturing into social forecasting. Furthermore, in practice this usually cannot be avoided because people must take some action today so that they will survive tomorrow. They do so by relying on their knowledge and experience; that is, they refer to the past.

Therefore it is incorrect to argue, as some scholars do, that "although [the] explanatory power [of historical factors] has been considerable, in analytical terms it can rarely be used as a basis for forecasts."[1] At the same time it is inaccurate to maintain that "anything is still possible" in Eastern Europe and, owing to that, the future course of political evolution in the region "cannot be foreseen."[2] Strictly speaking, a recurrence of communism, say, in the Czech Republic is possible; but who is going to assert that this is highly likely? If one claims that such a scenario is highly unlikely, then a forecast concerning the future political evolution of an East European state has already been made.

In most cases relating to public life, people are usually not much interested in all possible outcomes, since awareness of them is of little significance; instead, they are interested in likely ones because in practice they are the ones that matter most.

In reality, neither is "anything still possible," nor is this region "imprisoned by its own history,"[3] as some people argue. Were the latter indeed the case, then the future would become a simple extrapolation of the past, thereby eliminating change and, in that sense, history as we know it, since the future would repeat the past.

Times of revolutionary change make public life volatile and uncertain; to comprehend present turmoil, it is sometimes contended that "acquaintanceship with the past will serve you much better than a knowledge of recent events. Indeed, in this part of the world, to know the past—especially the distant past—is to understand the present."[4] In addition, it can be argued, knowing the past helps considerably to predict the immediate future.

Based on their varying knowledge of Eastern Europe, observers have varying views on the region's foreseeable future. Some argue that by the mid-1990s the Czech Republic, Hungary, and Poland were already "secure" democracies,[5] and this is an enduring metamorphosis. Others add Slovenia and Estonia to this category.[6] Yet some observers take an opposing view, maintaining that the region's democratic future is anything but bright. In their opinion, disappointment and bitterness are growing throughout Eastern Europe as hopes fade for a quick move to a market economy.[7] They contend that if the economic crisis in Eastern Europe persists or deepens, there is an acute danger that "social cohesion will be eroded, that nationalist tensions will mount and that civil wars may break out."[8]

Predicting the progress of Russia, the most important country of the region in global politics, is difficult; all or nearly all possible views have been expressed by now concerning its prospects for the foreseeable future. A typical Western opinion contains a large dose of skepticism regarding Moscow's likelihood of obtaining a durable democracy and a market economy without considerable assistance from the West. Experts contend that to see Russia accomplishing these goals by itself is most unlikely. Hence the conclusion is that "if the USA and the West disengage from Russia, authoritarianism will almost certainly take over, either by coup or by democratic election. Equally possible is chaos and civil war."[9]

More optimism is evident in regard to Poland and the Czech Republic. Some political analysts word opine that their future remains open-ended and distinguish five scenarios for at least the next twenty-five years. One observer believes that the systemic transformation may result in a populist-authoritarian regime, a laissez-faire state, a leaning-upon-the-West country, a sustainable development scenario, or a muddling-on case.[10] It can be argued, too, that some combination of these outcomes is probable as well.

Although most observers maintain that with the downfall of communism the danger to democracy or the market has disappeared, George Soros, a U.S. entrepreneur who has for many years promoted the ideals of open society throughout the world, came to the conclusion that the "international open society" itself may be its own "worst enemy."[11] He believes that the untrammeled intensification of laissez-faire capitalism and the spread of market values into all areas of life is endangering liberal democratic society.

For him, the main enemy of democracy is no longer the communist but the "capitalist threat." Under communism, the state repressed the freedom of the individual, whereas open society, that is, liberal democracy, suffers nowadays from the opposite—from "excessive individualism." This in turn may bring about too much competition and too little cooperation and thus can cause intolerable inequities and instability.

To substantiate his claim, Soros uses Russia as an example; in his view, the system of "robber capitalism" that has taken hold there is so iniquitous that its people may well turn to a charismatic leader promising national revival at the cost of civil liberties. That obviously spells the end of democracy for Russia. Despite this, the West has, according to him, failed to extend a helping hand to Moscow and Eastern Europe at large after the collapse of communism. As he put it: "The end of the Cold War brought a response very different from that at the end of World War II. The idea of a new Marshall Plan could not even be mooted. When I proposed such an idea at a conference in Potsdam, in the northern spring of 1989, I was literally laughed at."[12]

Soros's contention that the collapse of communism laid the groundwork for a universal open society but the Western democracies "failed" to rise to the occasion is debatable, however. His reasoning is based on the assumption that outsiders' help is crucial, even decisive, to establishing sustainable democracies and prosperous economies in the postcommunist countries of Eastern Europe. Left to themselves, these nations are doomed to failure; that is, they will not become a lasting part of the Western world in terms of political institutions and economic development.

His argument, however, does not stand up to close scrutiny. In all likelihood, it is not the West that will make or break the attainment of an enduring democracy and an affluent society for Eastern Europe. Its assistance, though important, is not decisive in this particular case. The frequently made comparison to U.S. aid given through the Marshall Plan to a Western Europe destroyed by war economies is misleading. It should be stressed repeatedly that this is not a case in point; the circumstances then differ drastically from the circumstances today.

The U.S. assistance to the West European countries helped them to rebuild market economies destroyed by war and to reestablish democracy, whereas the presently envisaged task is to establish them for the first time in almost every country of Eastern Europe. The difference is wide open and thereby difficult to overcome.

Although not always crystal clear to everyone else, this difference is, nonetheless, obvious to many former West Germans, who not so long ago were recipients of U.S. aid via the Marshall Plan and nowadays have turned into donors helping former communist East Germany in its efforts with systemic change. This unique opportunity gave them experience, empathy, insight into, and understanding of the problems involved in connection with fundamental transformation on a scale unparalleled elsewhere in the world. Unified in 1990, Germany consists of two radically different entities: a wealthy liberal democracy and a poor ex-communist country.

From the hitherto gathered experience regarding systemic change, Germans have become highly skeptical about being able to solve the political amd economic problems of the non-Western world through influx of capital alone. To illustrate, Helmut Schmidt, a former chancellor of West Germany, argues that a new

> Marshall Plan is hardly a model for a solution to the coming
> challenges of the developing world. Marshall aid was successful
> because [Western] Europe possessed a long standing en-
> trepreneurial heritage, a base of business acumen, a high level
> of general education and technological knowledge as well as
> engineering capabilities.[13]

His remarks referring to developing countries are even more pertinent to
the postcommunist states, which generally possess much less entrepreneurial tradition and business culture than many of those belonging
to the Third World.

If, then, outside assistance modeled on the Marshall Plan is not critical
for the nascent democracies and burgeoning market economies, what is it
that will make their progress toward sustainable, liberal, and wealthy
societies an ultimate success? The answer is that self-reliance, above all,
whether in the political domain or in the sphere of economics, is the crucial
factor. Furthermore, there must be a strong political will to attain these aims
coupled with the ability to do so; the latter is missing more often than not.
Ability, like capital, can be acquired; the problem is *how* to acquire it and
to acquire it quickly because time matters. Thus far nobody has come up
with a foolproof solution.

When the former chancellor of West Germany contended that material
assistance alone to developing countries is not enough to turn their backward economies into well functioning ones, he based his argument on their
past performance. For him the past matters with regard to predicting a likely
economic development in the foreseeable future.

It is only a seeming paradox to state that Russia in comparison to Poland
and the Czech Republic in particular made greater progress toward democracy and a market economy but still lags behind these two countries in this
respect. Notwithstanding Russia's impressive progress in the course of
systemic transformation, its starting point, in historical perspective, was
well behind that of its western neighbors because the country never in fact
experienced a democracy and very little of a market economy, either. Owing
predominantly to this, its chances of attaining these aims on a lasting basis
are still significantly smaller than the chances of the other two states and
uncertain as well. The timeframe is too short to make a prognosis with a
high degree of probability. The systemic change that began in Russia in the
early 1990s has not been completed as yet; hence its ultimate outcome
remains unclear. Although the international situation is currently very
conducive to democratic change and the establishment of a market econ-

omy, it is not in itself a decisive factor. A transformation along these lines is, in the final analysis, dependent on domestic sources.

Poland, which has had some experience of democracy, however little, is more likely for that reason to attain democracy now on a permanent basis. The same relates to a market economy; until World War II Poland's economy was grounded on private property, though the country had a backward, agricultural market economy judged by Western standards and without much competition. Since the demise of communism in the country, it has made greater progress toward establishing a sustainable democracy than a market economy largely because it is more familiar with the former than the latter. This should have been expected. In addition, introducing democratic institutions is relatively easier than introducing market mechanisms. For the latter to function effectively requires, all else being equal, a long span of time, perhaps several generations.

In one respect, at least, Poland and Russia are very much alike: both lack a liberal tradition. The concepts of compromise, tolerance, accommodation, and minority rights are alien to many people in these two countries. It is not a foregone conclusion that these concepts will now strike deep roots there, although the opportunity for this happening is much better today than ever before. For this to occur, the impact of the international environment is meaningful but not crucial. Again, much depends on domestic developments and the activity of the political elites in this sphere.

Among the three countries analyzed here, only the Czech Republic has extremely good chances of establishing *sustainable* liberal democracy and a market economy. Before the imposition of communism in the aftermath of World War II Czechoslovakia was already a democratic state, where liberal attitudes prevailed, with a modern, industrialized economy operating along market principles. As a result, the Czechs, unlike the Poles and the Russians, still possess experience and habits relevant to creating a liberal democratic society and a capitalist economy based on competition. Furthermore, the split of Czechoslovakia in 1993 into two independent states, the Czech Republic and Slovakia, enhanced the former's prospects of accomplishing these goals, since the latter has almost no experience of either a liberal democracy or a market economy, unlike the Czech lands now composing the Czech Republic. Also, there is much political will and determination among the Czech Republic leaders and the population at large to establish a liberal democratic polity together with a national economy grounded on widespread private property and market principles. Consensus politics, which is effectively practiced in that country, is absent in the other two states. Of course, the functioning of consensus of politics steps up the Czechs' prospects of enduringly establishing the envisaged aims.

Yet what makes the country's prospects even brighter, in comparison not only to Poland and Russia but perhaps to all other postcommunist states, is its approach to systemic change. Unlike the rest of the countries of the region, the Czech Republic decided to implement a comprehensive and rapid fundamental transformation based on the rule of law as well as on justice. By the time of this writing, that goal was attained to a large extent. This progress is what makes the difference between the Czech state and the remaining states of Eastern Europe. For such progress to have happened, the Czechs had to have previous experience. Other nations have had none or nearly none.

A relevant question to be posed here is whether there is an objective criterion for measuring the standard of living of an average citizen in a given country. Yes, there are, in fact, numerous criteria. All of them were invented by economists, and perhaps because of that they are costly, time-consuming, and unreliable. In contrast, the method suggested here is cheap, fast, and foolproof: Upon arrival in an East European country, a visitor should find out whether its people are punctual and the public toilets clean—an unmistakable sign of a high standard of living if they are. Believe it or not, punctuality and cleanliness are linked closely to the high standards of living of contemporary society.

NOTES

1. For instance, László Csaba, *The Capitalist Revolution in Eastern Europe: A Contribution to the Economic Theory of Systemic Change* (Aldershot, England: Edward Elgar, 1995), p. 291.

2. Sten Berglund and Jan Åke Dellenbrant, "The Evolution of Party Systems in Eastern Europe," *Journal of Communist Studies*, Vol. 8, No. 1, March 1992, p. 158.

3. Johnathan Sunley, "Post-Communism: An Infantile Disorder," *The National Interest,* No. 44, summer 1996, p. 3.

4. Ibid.

5. *Newsweek*, 9 December 1996, p. 17.

6. See, for instance, Zbigniew Brzezinski, "The Stages of Postcommunist Transformation," in Yevhen Bystrycky et al. (eds.), *The Political Analysis of Postcommunism* (Kiev: Political Thought, 1995), p. 117.

7. Leif Rosenberger, "Economic Transition in Eastern Europe: Paying the Price for Freedom," *East European Quarterly*, Vol. 26, No. 3, September 1992, p. 261.

8. See, for instance, Friedrich Levcik, "Economic Transformation in the East: A Critical Appraisal of Its Development and Suggestions for a Possible Way Out," in Christopher T. Saunders (ed.), *Eastern Europe in Crisis and the Way Out* (London: Macmillan, 1995), p. 26.

9. Ariel Cohen, "Aid Russia, but Reform the U.S. Program," *Problems of Post-Communism*, Vol. 42, No. 3, May-June 1995, p. 32.

10. See, for instance, Hans von Zon, "Alternative Scenarios for Central Europe," in Jerzy Hausner, Bob Jessop, and Klaus Nielsen (eds.), *Strategic Choice and Path-Dependency in Post-Socialism* (Aldershot, England: Edward Elgar, 1995), p. 116.

11. *The Weekend Australian*, March 8–9. 1997.

12. Ibid.

13. *The Australian*, 2 June 1997.

Selected Bibliography

Adam, Jan. "Transformation to a Market Economy in the Former Czechoslovakia," *Europe-Asia Studies*, Vol. 45, No. 4, 1993, pp. 627–646.

The Age, 31 May 1997.

Amsden, Alice H.; Kochanowicz, Jacek; and Taylor, Lance. *The Market Meets Its Match: Restructuring the Economies of Eastern Europe*. Cambridge, MA: Harvard University Press, 1994.

Aron, Leon. "Boris Yeltsin and Russia's Four Crises," *Journal of Democracy*, Vol. 4, No. 2, 1993, pp. 4–16.

Åslund, Anders. "The Case for Radical Reform," *Journal of Democracy*, Vol. 5, No. 4, October 1994, pp. 62–74.

———. "Niektóre wnioski z pierwszych czterech lat transformacji," in Marek Dabrowski (ed.), *Polityka gospodarcza okresu transformacji*. Warsaw: PWN, 1995, pp. 361–377.

The Australian. 7 March 1997.

The Australian. 15 May 1997.

The Australian. 16 May 1997.

The Australian. 26 May 1997.

The Australian. 28 May 1997.

The Australian. 29 May 1997.

The Australian. 2 June 1997.

Bachman, Klaus. "Poland," in Hanspeter Neuhold, Peter Havlik, and Arnold Suppan (eds.), *Political and Economic Transformation in East Central Europe*. Boulder, CO: Westview Press, 1995, pp. 37–56.

Barberis, Nicholas; Boycko, Maxim; Shleifer, Andrei; and Tsukanova, Natalia. "How Does Privatization Work? Evidence from the Russian Shops," *Journal of Political Economy*, Vol. 14, No. 4, August 1996, pp. 764–790.

Barry, Norman. "The Social Market Economy," in Ellen Fränkel Paul, Fred D. Miller, Jr., and Jeffrey Paul (eds.), *Liberalism and the Economic Order*. Cambridge: Cambridge University Press, 1993, pp. 1–25.

Berend, Ivan T. "Alternatives of Transformation: Choices and Determinants: East-Central Europe in the 1990s," in Beverley Crawford (ed.), *Markets, States and Democracy: The Political Economy of Postcommunist Transformation*. Boulder, CO: Westview Press, 1995, pp. 130–149.

Berglund, Sten; and Dellenbrant, Jan Åke. "The Evolution of Party Systems in Eastern Europe," *Journal of Communist Studies*, Vol. 8, No. 1, March 1992, pp. 148–159.

Birgerson, Susanne M.; and Kanet, Roger E. "East-Central Europe and the Russian Federation," *Problems of Post-Communism*, Vol. 42, No. 4, July-August 1995, pp. 29–36.

Birman, Igor. "Gloomy Prospects for the Russian Economy," *Europe-Asia Studies*, Vol. 48, No. 5, July 1996, pp. 735–750.

Bocheński, Aleksander. *Rzecz o psychice narodu polskiego*. Warsaw: Państwowy Instytut Wydawniczy, ŇýňŇ.

Brzezinski, Zbign6iew. "The Stages of Postcommunist Transformation," in Yevhen Bystrycky et al. (eds.), *The Political Analysis of Postcommunism*. Kiev: Political Thought, 1995, pp. 103–117.

Burke, Edmund. *Reflections on the Revolution in France*. Boston: Little, Brown, 1901.

Burke, Justine. "Russia's Curse: Weak Political Institutions Unable to Restrain Arbitrary Leadership," *Demokratizatsya*, Vol. 4, No. 3, summer 1996, pp. 330–340.

Campbell, Robert W. "Evaluating Russian Economic Reform: A Review Essay," *Post-Soviet Affairs*, Vol. 12, No. 2, April-June 1996, pp. 181–193.

Cepl, Vojtěch; and Gillis, Mark. "Making Amends after Communism," *Journal of Democracy*, Vol. 7, No. 4, October 1996, pp. 118–124.

Chavance, Bernard. *The Transformation of Communist Systems: Economic Reforms since the 1950s*. Boulder, CO: Westview Press, 1994.

Chrościcki, Tadeusz. "Przebieg Procesów Społeczno-Gospodarczych w Latach 1990–95. Próba Oceny," in *Transformacje polskiej gospodarki w latach 1990–95*. Warsaw: Instytut Rozwoju i Studiów Strategicznych, 1996, pp. 6–61.

Clark, John; and Wildavsky, Aaron. *The Moral Collapse of Communism: Poland as a Cautionary Tale*. San Francisco: ICS Press, 1990.

Cohen, Ariel. "Aid Russia, but Reform the U.S. Program," *Problems of Post-Communism*, Vol. 42, No. 3, May-June 1995, pp. 32–35.

Country Profile: Czech Republic. London: Economist Intelligence Unit, 1996.

Country Profile: Poland. London: Economist Intelligence Unit, 3rd quarter 1996.

Country Profile: Russia, 1994–1995. London: Economist Intelligence Unit, 1995.

Country Report: Russia. London: Economist Intelligence Unit, 3rd quarter 1996.

Crawford, Beverley. "Post-Communist Political Economy: A Framework for the Analysis of Reform," in Beverly Crawford (ed.), *Markets, States and Democracy: The Political Economy of Post-communist Transformation*. Boulder, CO: Westview Press, 1995, pp. 3–42.

Csaba, László. *The Capitalist Revolution in Eastern Europe: A Contribution to the Economic Theory of Systemic Change*. Aldershot, England: Edward Elgar, 1995.

————. "The Political Economy of the Reform Strategy: China and Eastern Europe Compared," *Communist Economies and Economic Transformation*, Vol. 8, No. 1, March 1996, pp. 53–65.

Dahl, Robert A. "The Problem of Civic Competence," Journal of Democracy, Vol. 3, No. 4, October 1992, pp. 45–59.

————. "Why Free Markets Are Not Enough," *Journal of Democracy*, Vol. 3, No. 3, July 1992, pp. 82–89.

Dahrendorf, Ralph. *Reflections on the Revolution in Europe*. New York: Times Books, Random House, 1990.

Darbellay, Alina. "Farmers and Entrepreneurs in Poland and the Czech Republic," *Transition*, Vol. 2, No. 15, July 1996, pp. 17–21.

Donnorummo, Roberto. "Poland's Political and Economic Transition," *East European Quarterly*, Vol. 18, No. 2, June 1994, pp. 259–280.

Dyba, Karel; and Svejnar, Jan. Chapter 2 in Jan Svejnar (ed.), *The Czech Republic and Economic Transition in Eastern Europe*. San Diego, CA: Academic Press, 1995, pp. 21–45.

The Economist. 21 September 1991.

The Economist. 26 October—1 November 1996.

Ekiert, Grzegorz. "Peculiarities of Post-Communist Politics: The Case of Poland," *Studies in Comparative Communism*, Vol. 25, No. 4, December 1992, pp. 341–361.

Fischer-Galati, Stephen. "The Political Right in Eastern Europe in Historical Perspective," in Joseph Held (ed.), *Democracy and Right-Wing Politics in Eastern Europe in the 1990's*. Boulder, CO: East European Monographs, 1993, pp. 1–12.

Fish, M. Steven. *Democracy from Scratch: Opposition and Regime in the New Russian Revolution*. Princeton, NJ: Princeton University Press, 1995.

Fivonen, Jyrki. "Russian Political Development and Prospects," in Timo Pürainen (ed.), *Change and Continuity in Eastern Europe*. Aldershot, England: Dartmouth, 1994, pp. 31–59.

Flakierski, Henryk. "Market Socialism Revisited: An Alternative for Eastern Europe," *International Journal of Sociology*, Vol. 25, No. 3, fall 1995, pp. 5–95.

Fogel, Daniel S.; and Etcheverry, Suzanne. "Performing the Economics of Central and Eastern Europe," in Daniel S. Fogel (ed.), *Managing in Emerging Market Economies*. Boulder, CO: Westview Press, 1994, pp. 3–33.

Frydman, Roman; Murphy, Kenneth; and Rapaczynski, Andrzej. "Capitalism with a Comrade's Face," *Transition*, Vol. 2, No. 2, 26 January 1996, pp. 5-11.

Fukuyama, Francis. "The Primacy of Culture," *Journal of Democracy*, Vol. 6, No. 1, January 1995, pp. 7–14.

Gazeta Bankowa. 18 August 1996.

Gazeta Wyborcza. 7 August 1996.

Gazeta Wyborcza. 19 December 1996.

De George, Richard T. "Scientific Capitalism: The Stage after Communism," *Problems of Post-Communism*, Vol. 42, No. 3, May-June 1995, pp. 15–18.

Geremek, Bronisław. "A Horizon of Hope and Fear," *Journal of Democracy*, Vol. 4, No. 3, 1993, pp. 100–105.

Goldman, Marshall; and Kapstein, Ethan B. "Economic Conversion in Perspective," *Demokratizatsyia*, Vol. 4, No. 1, winter 1996, pp. 55–68.

Gomułka, Stanisław. "Economic and Political Constraints during Transition," *Europe-Asia Studies*, Vol. 46, No. 1, 1994, pp. 89–106.

————. "The IMF-supported Programs of Poland and Russia, 1990–1994: Principles, Errors, and Results," *Journal of Comparative Economics*, No. 20, 1995, pp. 316–346.

————. "Polish Economic Reform, 1990–1991: Principles, Policies and Outcomes," *Cambridge Journal of Economics*, No. 16, 1992, pp. 355–372.

Grahm, Carol. "The Polities of Safety Nets," *Journal of Democracy*, Vol. 6, No. 2, April 1995, pp. 142–156.

Gurushina, Natalia; and Szilagyi, Zsofia. "Seeking Foreign Investment in Hungary and Russia," *Transition*, Vol. 1, No. 2, 26 January 1996, pp. 22–25.

Haddad, Louis. "On the Rational Sequencing of Enterprise Reform," *Journal of Communist Studies and Transitional Politics*, Vol. 11, No. 1, March 1995, pp. 91–109.

Hausner, Jerzy; Jessop, Bob; and Nielsen, Klaus (eds.). *Strategic Choice and Path-Dependency in Post-Socialism*. Aldershot, England: Edward Elgar, 1995.

Havel, Vaclav; Klaus, Vaclav; and Pithart, Petr. "Civil Society after Communism: Rival Visions," *Journal of Democracy*, Vol. 7, No. 1, January 1996, pp. 12–23.

Hedlund, Stefan; and Sundström, Niclas. "The Russian Economy after Systemic Change," *Europe-Asia Studies*, Vol. 48, No. 6, September 1996, pp. 887–914.

Hellman, Joel. "Constitutions and Economic Reform in the Postcommunist Transitions," *East European Constitutional Review*, Vol. 5, No. 1, winter 1996, pp. 45–56.

Henderson, Anne. "The Politics of Foreign Investment in Eastern Europe: Lessons from the Polish and Hungarian Experiences," *Problems of Post-Communism*, Vol. 42, No. 3, May-June 1995, pp. 51–56.

Hermann-Pilath, Carsten. "Systemic Transformation as an Economic Problem," *Aussen Politik*, Vol. 42, No. 2, 1992, pp. 171–182.

Hernàndez-Catà, Ernesto. "Russia and the IMF: The Political Economy of Macro-Stabilization," *Problems of Post-Communism*, Vol. 42, No. 3, May-June 1995, pp. 19–26.

Herring, Eric. "International Security and Democratisation in Eastern Europe," in Geoffrey Pridham, Eric Herring, and George Sandford (eds.), *Building Democracy? The International Dimension of Democratisation in Eastern Europe*. London: Leicester University Press, 1994, pp. 87–118.

Holy, Ladislav. *The Little Czech and the Great Czech Nation: National Identity and the Post-Communist Transformation of Society*. Cambridge: Cambridge University Press, 1996.

Horowitz, Donald L. "Democracy in Divided Societies," *Journal of Democracy*, Vol. 4, No. 4, October 1993, pp. 18–38.

Hosking, Geoffrey. "Surviving Communism," *Index on Censorship*, Vol. 25, No. 3, May-June 1996, pp. 38–43.

Hume, David. *An Inquiry Concerning Human Understanding*. Indianapolis: Liberal Arts Press, 1995.

Huntington, Samuel P. "Democracy's Third Wave," *Journal of Democracy*, Vol. 2, No. 2, spring 1991, pp. 3–34.

Hunya, Gabor. "A Progress Report on Privatisation in Eastern Europe," in Christopher T. Saunders (ed.), *Eastern Europe in Crisis and the Way Out*. London: Macmillan, 1995, pp. 281–310.

Hyde-Price, Adrian G. V. "Democratization in Eastern Europe: The External Dimension," in Geoffrey Pridham and Tatu Vanhaneu (eds.), *Democratization in Eastern Europe: Domestic and International Perspectives*. London: Routledge, 1994, pp. 220–252.

Janos, Andrew. "Continuity and Change in Eastern Europe: Strategies of Post-Communist Politics," in Beverley Crawford (ed.), *Markets, States and Democracy: The Political Economy of Post-Communist Transformation*. Boulder, CO: Westview Press, 1955, pp. 150–174.

Johnson, Simon. "Private Business in Eastern Europe," in Oliver Jean Blanchard, Kenneth A. Frost, and Jeffrey D. Sachs (eds.), *The Transition in Eastern Europe*, Vol. 2. Chicago: University of Chicago Press, 1994, pp. 245–292.

Jowitt, Ken. "Undemocratic Past, Unnamed Present, Undecided Future," *Demokratizatsya*, Vol. 4, No. 3, summer 1996, pp. 409–419.

Keman, Hans. "Managing the Mixed Economy in Central and Eastern Europe: Democratic Politics and the Role of the Public Sector," *Democratization*, Vol. 3, No. 2, summer 1996, pp. 92–114.

Kennedy, Michael D; and Gianoplus, Pauline. "Entrepreneurs and Expertise: A Cultural Encounter in the Making of Post-Communist Capitalism in Poland," *East European Politics and Societies*, Vol. 8, No. 1, winter 1994, pp. 58–93.

Klaus, Vaclav. "Transition—An Insider's View," *Problems of Communism*, Vol. 41, Nos. 1–2, January-April 1992, pp. 73–75.

Kober, Stanley. "The French Revolution, the American Revolution, and Russia Today," *Problems of Post-Communism*, Vol. 42, No. 5, September-October 1995, pp. 50–53.

Kojder, Andrzej. "Corruption in Poland Today," *Polish Sociological Bulletin*, Nos. 3–4 (99–100), 1992, pp. 329–343.

Kontorovich, Vladimir. "Imperial Legacy and the Transformation of the Russian Economy," *Transition*, Vol. 2, No. 27, 23 August 1996, pp. 22–25.

Kopecki, Peter. "Developing Party Organizations in East-Central Europe," *Party Politics*, Vol. 1, No. 4, 1995, pp. 515–534.

Kopstein, Jeffrey. "Weak Foundations under East German Reconstruction," *Transition*, Vol. 2, No. 2, 26 January 1996, pp. 34–36.

Korbonski, Andrzej. "How Much Is Enough? Excessive Pluralism as the Cause of Poland's Socio-Economic Crisis," *International Political Science Review*, Vol. 17, No. 3, July 1996, pp. 297–306.

Kornai, Janos. "Transformation Recession: The Example of Hungary," in Christopher T. Saunders (ed.), *Eastern Europe in Crisis and the Way Out*. London: Macmillan, 1995, pp. 29–77.

Kovacs, Dezso; and Maggard, Sally Ward. "The Human Face of Political, Economic, and Social Change in Eastern Europe," *East European Quarterly*, Vol. 27, No. 3, September 1993, pp. 317–349.

Kowalik, Tadeusz. "The Free Market or a Social Contract as Bases for Systemic Transformation," in Jerzy Hausner, Bob Jessop, and Klaus Nielsen (eds.), *Strategic Choice and Path-Dependency in Post-Socialism*. Aldershot, England: Edward Elgar, 1995, pp. 131–148.

———. "On the Transformation of Post-Communist Societies: The Inefficiency of Primitive Capital Accumulation," *International Political Science Review*, Vol. 17, No. 3, July 1996, pp. 289–296.

Kramer, Mark. "Polish Workers and the Post-Communist Transition, 1989–93," *Europe-Asia Studies*, Vol. 47, No. 4, 1995, pp. 669–712.

Krol, Marcin. "Poland's Longing for Paternalism," *Journal of Democracy*, Vol. 5, No. 1, January 1994, pp. 85–95.

Krug, Barbara. "Blood, Sweat, or Cheating: Politics and the Transformation of Socialist Economies in China, the USSR, and Eastern Europe," *Studies in Comparative Communism*, Vol. 24, No. 2, June 1991, pp. 137–150.

Kryshtanovskaya, Olga; and White, Stephen. "From Soviet Nomenklatura to Russian Elite," *Europe-Asia Studies*, Vol. 48, No. 5, July 1996, pp. 711–733.

Leach, Jerry W. "The Emergence of Private Farming in Russia," *Problems of Post-Communism*, Vol. 42, No. 4, July-August 1995, pp. 47–52.

Levcik, Friedrich. "Economic Transformation in the East: A Critical Appraisal of Its Development and Suggestions for a Possible Way Out," in Christopher T. Saunders (ed.), *Eastern Europe in Crisis and the Way Out*. London: Macmillan, 1995, pp. 13–28.

Lewis, Paul. "Civil Society and the Development of Political Parties in East-Central Europe," *The Journal of Communist Studies*, Vol. 9, No. 4, December 1993, pp. 5–20.

Lewis, Paul G. "Political Institutionalisation and Party Development in Post-Communist Poland," *Europe-Asia Studies*, Vol. 46, No. 5, 1994, pp. 779–799.

Lewis, Paul; Lomax, Bill; and Wightman, Gordon. "The Emergence of Multi-Party Systems in East-Central Europe: A Comparative Analysis," in Geoffrey Pridham and Tatu Vanhaven (eds.), *Democratization in Eastern Europe: Domestic and International Perspectives*. London: Routledge, 1994, pp. 151–188.

Lomax, Bill. "Impediments to Democratization in Post-Communist East-Central Europe," in Gordon Wightman (ed.), *Party Formation in East-Central Europe*. Aldershot, England: Edward Elgar, 1995, pp. 179–201.

Major, Ivan. "The Decay of the Command Economics," *Eastern European Politics and Societies*, Vol. 8, No. 2, spring 1994, pp. 317–357.

Maravall, Jose Maria. "The Myth of the Authoritarian Advantage," *Journal of Democracy*, Vol. 5, No. 4, October 1994, pp. 17–32.

Markowski, Stefan; and Sharon Jackson. "The Attractiveness of Poland to Direct Foreign Investors," *Communist Economies and Economic Transformation*, Vol. 6, No. 4, 1994, pp. 515–535.

Mathijs, Erik; and Swinnen, Jo. "Agricultural Privatization and De-Collectivization in Central and Eastern Europe," *Transition*, Vol. 2, No. 5, 26 July 1996, pp. 12–16.

Mertlik, Pavel. "Transformation of the Czech and Slovak Economies, 1990–92: Design, Problems, Costs," in Jerzy Hausner, Bob Jessop, and Klaus Nielsen (eds.), *Strategic Choice and Path-Dependency in Post-Socialism*. Aldershot, England: Edward Elgar, 1995, pp. 218–229.

Michnik, Adam. "Testament of Lies," *Index on Censorship*, Vol. 25, No. 5, September-October 1996, pp. 145–147.

Michnik, Adam; and Havel, Vaclav. "Justice or Revenge?" *Journal of Democracy*, Vol. 4, No. 1, January 1993, pp. 20–27.

Millar, James. "From Utopian Socialism to Utopian Capitalism: The Failure of Revolution and Reform in Post-Soviet Russia," in Timo Pürainen (ed.), *Change and Continuity in Eastern Europe*. Aldershot, England: Dartmouth, 1994, pp. 7–14.

Molchanov, Mikhail A. "Russian Neo-Communism: Autocracy, Orthodoxy, Nationality," *The Harriman Review*, Vol. 9, No. 3, summer 1996, pp. 69–79.

Myant, Martin. "Economic Reform and Political Evolution in Eastern Europe," *Journal of Communist Studies*, Vol. 8, No. 1, March 1992, pp. 107–127.

Nagengast, Emil. "Eastern Europe and Germany's Treuhandanstalt," *East European Quarterly*, Vol. 29, No. 2, June 1995, pp. 189–206.

The New York Times. 15 October 1996.

The New York Times. 9 November 1996.

The New York Times. 11 November 1996.

The New York Times. 16 November 1996.

The New York Times. 12 December 1996.

The New York Times. 17 December 1996.

The New York Times. 25 December 1996.

Newsweek. 9 December 1996.

Ordeshook, Peter C. "Russia's Party System: Is Russian Federalism Viable?" *Post-Soviet Affairs*, Vol. 12, No. 3, July-September 1996, pp. 195–217.

Orenstein, Mitchell. "The Failures of Neo-Liberal Social Policy in Central Europe," *Transition*, Vol. 2, No. 13, 28 June 1996, pp. 16–20.

Orłowski, Witold M. "Kulejacy tygrys," *Gazeta Bankowa*, 1 September 1996, p. 18.

Orttung, Robert W.; and Anna Paretskaya. "Presidential Election Demonstrates Rural-Urban Divide," *Transition*, Vol. 2, No. 19, 20 September 1996, pp. 33–38.

Palma, Giuseppe Di. "Why Democracy Can Work in Eastern Europe," *Journal of Democracy*, Vol. 2, No. 1, winter 1991, pp. 21–31.

Pareto, Vilfredo. *The Transformation of Democracy* (edited with an introduction by Charles H. Powers). New Brunswick, NJ: Transaction Books, 1984.

Parland, Thomas. *The Rejection in Russia of Totalitarian Socialism and Liberal Democracy: A Study of the Russian New Right*. Helsinki: Finnish Society of Sciences and Letters, 1993.

Peng, Yali. "Privatization in Eastern Europe Countries," *East Europe Quarterly*, Vol. 26, No. 4, January 1993, pp. 471–484.

Perlez, Jane. "For Hungarian Army Officers, It's 'Eyes West' " *The New York Times*, 2 January 1997.

Pinder, John. "The European Community and Democracy in Central and Eastern Europe," in Geoffrey Pridham, Eric Herring, and George Sanford (eds.), *Building Democracy? The International Dimension of Democratisation in Eastern Europe*. London: Leicester University Press, 1994, pp. 119–143.

Poland: Country Report. 2nd quarter 1996. London: Economist Intelligence Unit, 1996.

Poland: 1995–96. London: Economist Intelligence Unit, 1996.

Polityka. 31 July 1993.

Polityka. 10 August 1996.

Polityka. 5 October 1996.

Polityka. 12 October 1996.

Pond, Elizabeth. "Poland Is Not Yugoslavia. Neither Is Ukraine," *The Harriman Review*, Vol. 8, No. 2, July 1995, pp. 1–4.

Poznanski, Kazimierz Z. "Political Economy of Privatization in Eastern Europe," in Jerzy Hausner, Bob Jessop, and Klaus Nielsen (eds.), *Strategic Choice and Path-Defendency in Post-Socialism*. Aldershot, England: Edward Elger, 1995.

Pridham, Geoffrey. "The International Dimension of Democratisation: Theory, Practice, and Inter-Regional Comparisons," in Geoffrey Pridham, Eric Herring, and George Sanford (eds.), *Building Democracy? The International Dimension of Democratisation in Eastern Europe*. London: Leicester University Press, 1994, pp. 7–31.

Prybyla, Jan S. "The Road from Socialism: Why, Where, What and How?" *Problems of Communism*, Vol. 40, Nos. 1–2, January-April 1991, pp. 1–17.

"Prywatyzacja. Z Józefem Kowalczykiem wiceministrem, przekształceń własnośaciowych rozmawia Małgorzata Pokojska," *Życie Gospodarcze*, 30 August 1996, pp. 29–31.

Przeglad Tygodniowy. 18 September 1996.

Przeworski, Adam. *Democracy and the Market: Political and Economic Reforms in Eastern Europe and Latin America*. Cambridge: Cambridge University Press, 1991.

Radu, Michael. "Western Diasporas in Post-Communist Transitions," *Problems of Post-Communism*, Vol. 42, No. 3, May-June 1995, pp. 57–62.

Remnick, David. "Can Russia Change?" *Foreign Affairs*, Vol. 76, No. 1, January-February 1997, pp. 35–49.

Review of Agricultural Policies: Czech Republic. Paris: Organization for Economic Cooperation and Development, 1995.

Riley, Patrick (ed.). *Leibniz: Political Writings*. Cambridge: Cambridge University Press, 1972.

Roesler, Jorg. "Privatization in Eastern Germany—Experience with the Treuhand," *Europe-Asia Studies*, Vol. 46, No. 3, 1994, pp. 505–517.

Rondinelli, Dennis A.; and Yurkiewicz, Jay. "Privatization and Economic Restructuring in Poland: An Assessment of Transition Policies," *American*

Journal of Economics and Sociology, Vol. 55, No. 2, April 1996, pp. 145–160.

Rose, Richard. "Mobilizing Demobilized Voters in Post-Communist Societies," *Party Politics,* Vol. 1, No. 4, 1995, pp. 549–563.

————. "Postcommunism and the Problem of Trust," *Journal of Democracy,* Vol. 5, No. 3, July 1994, pp. 18–30.

Rosenberger, Leif. "Economic Transition in Eastern Europe: Paying the Price for Freedom," *East European Quarterly,* Vol. 26, No. 3, September 1992, pp. 261–278.

Roskin, Michael G. "The Emerging Party Systems of Central and Eastern Europe," *East European Quarterly,* Vol. 27, No. 1, March 1993, pp. 47–63.

"Rozmowa z Miltonem i Rose Friedmanami," *Wprost,* No. 32, 11 August 1996, pp. 17–18.

Russian Economic Trends. Vol. 5, No. 2, 1996.

Russian Economic Trends: Monthly Update. 22 October 1996.

Rutland, Peter. "Russia's Unsteady Entry into the Global Economy," *Current History,* Vol. 95, No. 603, October 1996, pp. 322–329.

Rychetnik, Ludek. "Can the Czech Republic Develop a Negotiated Economy?" in Jerzy Hausner, Bob Jessop, and Klaus Nielsen (eds.), *Strategic Choice and Path-Dependency in Post-Socialism.* Aldershot, England: Edward Elgar, 1995, pp. 230–258.

Sachs, Jeffrey. *Poland's Jump to the Market Economy.* Cambridge, MA: MIT Press, 1993.

Sakwa, Richard. "The Struggle for the Constitution in Russia and the Triumph of Ethical Individualism," *Studies in East European Thought,* Vol. 48, Nos. 2–4, September 1996, pp. 115–157.

Sartori, Giovanni. "How Far Can Free Government Travel?" *Journal of Democracy,* Vol. 6, No. 3, July 1995, pp. 101–111.

Schulz, Fryderyk. *Podróże Inflantczyka z Rygi do Warszawy i po Polsce w latach 1791–1793.* Warsaw: Czytelnik, 1956.

Shapiro, Ian. "Elements of Democratic Justice," *Political Theory,* Vol. 24, No. 4, November 1996, pp. 579–619.

Shishkov, Iu. "Russia's Thorny Path to the Global Economy," *Russian Social Science Review,* Vol. 3, No. 6, November-December 1996, pp. 3–19.

Siklova, Jirina. "Lustration or the Czech Way of Screening," *East European Constitutional Review,* Vol. 5, No. 1, winter 1996, pp. 57–62.

Starovoitova, Galina. "Weimar Russia?" *Journal of Democracy,* Vol. 4, No. 3, 1993, pp. 106–109.

Stokes, Susan C. "Public Opinion and Market Reforms: The Limits of Economic Voting," *Comparative Political Studies,* Vol. 29, No. 5, October 1996, pp. 499–519.

Sunley, Johnathan. "Post-Communism: An Infantile Disorder," *The National Interest*, No. 44, summer 1996, pp. 3–15.

Sztompka, Piotr. "The Intangibles and Imponderables of the Transition to Democracy," *Studies in Comparative Communism*, Vol. 24, No. 3, September 1991, pp. 295–311.

————. "Looking Back: The Year 1989 as a Cultural and Civilizational Break," *Communist and Post-Communist Studies*, Vol. 29, No. 2, June 1996, pp. 115–130.

Tamasi, Peter. "The Role of Social Sciences in the Central and East European Transformation Process," *International Social Science Journal*, No. 148, June 1996, pp. 269–276.

Taranovski, Theodore. "The Problem of Reform in Russian and Soviet History," in Theodore Taranovski (ed.), *Reform in Modern Russian History: Progress or Cycle?* New York and Cambridge: Woodrow Wilson Center Press and Cambridge University Press, 1995, pp. 1–24.

Taras, Ray. "The End of the Wałesa Era in Poland," *Current History*, Vol. 95, No. 599, March 1996, pp. 124–128.

Teichova, Alice. *The Czechoslovak Economy, 1918–1980*. London: Routledge, 1988.

The Times. 24 September 1996.

Tocqueville, Alexis de. *Democracy in America*. New York: New American Library, 1956.

Torańska, Teresa. *My*. Warsaw: Oficyna Wydawnicza MOST, 1994.

Trzeciakowski, Witold. "Transition in Poland," in Christopher T. Saunders (ed.), *Eastern Europe in Crisis and the Way Out*. London: Macmillan, 1995, pp. 422–450.

Tucker, Aviezer. "Wrestling the Entrenched Education Bureaucracy," *Transition*, Vol. 2, No. 12, 14 January 1996, pp. 46–47.

Upława, Stanisław. "Główne Problemy Transformacji Polskiej Gospodarki. Co. wynika z badan IRISS?" in *Transformacje polskiej gospodarki, w latach 1990–95*. Warsaw: Instytut Rozwojui Studiów Strategicznych, 1996.

Varoli, John D. "There Are More 'New Poor' than 'New Russians,' " *Transition*, Vol. 2, No. 2, 4 October 1996, pp. 6–11.

Waller, J. Michael. "The KGB Legacy in Russia," *Problems of Post-Communism*, Vol. 42, No. 6, November-December 1995, pp. 3–10.

The Warsaw Voice. 8 September 1996.

The Warsaw Voice. 22 September 1996.

Weber, Max. *The Protestant Ethic and the Spirit of Capitalism*. New York: Routledge, 1930.

Wedel, Janine. "U.S. Aid to Central and Eastern Europe: Results and Recommendations," *Problems of Post-Communism*, Vol. 42, No. 3, May-June 1995, pp. 45–50.

The Weekend Australian. 8–9 March 1997.

The Weekend Australian. 15–16 March 1997.

The Weekend Australian. 31 May–1 June 1997.

Wegren, Stephen K. "Rural Reform and Political Culture in Russia," *Europe-Asia Studies*, Vol. 46, No. 2, 1994, pp. 215–241.

Werning Rivera, Sharon. "Historical Cleavages or Transition Mode? Influence on the Emerging Party Systems in Poland, Hungary and Czechoslovakia," *Party Politics*, Vol. 2, No. 2, April 1996, pp. 177–208.

White, Stephen. "Post-Communist Politics: Towards Democratic Pluralism?" *Journal of Communist Studies*, Vol. 9, No. 1, March 1993, pp. 18–32.

Will, Gary (ed.). *The Federalist Papers by Alexander Hamilton, James Madison and John Jay*. New York: Bantam Books, 1982; first published in 1787–88.

Winiecki, Jan. "The Polish Transition Programme: Underpinnings, Results, Interpretations," *Soviet Studies*, Vol. 44, No. 5, 1992, pp. 809–835.

Wolchik, Sharon L. *Czechoslovakia in Transition: Politics, Economics and Society*. London: Pinter Publishers, 1991.

Wprost. 25 August 1996.

Wprost. 1 September 1996.

Zadornov, Mikhail. Public lecture, Melbourne University, Melbourne, 25 February 1997.

Zhelev, Zhelyu. "Is Communism Returning?" *Journal of Democracy*, Vol. 7, No. 3, July 1996, pp. 3–6.

Zielonka, Jan. "New Institutions in the Old East Bloc," *Journal of Democracy*, Vol. 5, No. 2, April 1994, pp. 87–104.

Zon, Hans von. "Alternative Scenarios for Central Europe," in Jerzy Hausner, Bob Jessop, and Klaus Nielsen (eds.), *Strategic Choice and Path-Dependency in Post-Socialism*. Aldershot, England: Edward Elgar, 1995, pp. 84–112.

Index

Abortion, 77
Accountability, 54, 77
Agency for International Development (USAID), 129
Agriculture: in the Czech Republic, 88, 100–101, 113–14; in Poland, 86, 88; privatization of, 51, 57; in Russia, 49, 51, 62–63, 113
Albania, 4, 123
Alekperov, Vagit, 67
American University, 129

Apparatchiks, 39
Asian economic change, 35, 37
Authoritarian regimes, 19–22, 34–35, 37, 50–51

Bielecki, Jan Krzysztof, 76
Bismarck, Otto Von, 6
Bolshevik revolution, 50
Brzezinski, Zbigniew, 124
Bureau for Europe and the New Independent States, 129

Capital flight, 56, 61, 125, 134
Capital investment, 64, 89, 112–13, 121, 124–25, 139
Capitalism, 28–29, 105, 143. *See also* Market economy; Transition to market economy
Catherine the Great, 50–51
Censorship in Russia, 53
Central Europe, 16
Charter 77, 103
Chechnya, 122
Chernomyrdin, Viktor, 56, 67
China, 134
Christian Democratic Party, 104
Christian Orthodox Church, 5
Chubais, Anatoly, 58
Church and state, 5, 26, 28, 53, 76–78
Civic Democratic Party, 103
Civic Forum, 103
Civic Movement, 103
Civil society as prerequisite to democracy, 35, 38–39, 52–53, 76. *See also* Personal values

Clinton, Bill, 133
Communist parties, 58, 79, 99, 102–3
Competition, 24, 28–29, 35–36, 61, 82, 105–6
Compromise, 26, 55, 78
Constituent Assembly (Russia), 51
Constitutions, 52, 72, 74, 77, 83
Corruption in government, 54–56, 64, 67, 75–76, 82, 110
Criminal organizations in Russia, 55–56
Czechoslovakia, 30, 107
Czech Republic, 97–115; agriculture in, 88, 100–101, 113–14; communist parties in, 15, 99, 102–3; corruption in, 110; decommunization in, 108–9; democracy in, 142–43, 146–47; ethnic conflict in, 108; foreign assistance to, 136; foreign investment in, 89, 112–13, 130, 135, 139; formation of, 107–8; inflation in, 99; justice and fairness in, 81, 109–10; media perception of, 97–98; North Atlantic Treaty Organization and, 133–34; personal values in, 105–6, 109–10; political parties in, 102–3; privatization in, 86, 88, 112–13; rise in expectations in, 106–7; role of precommunist past in, 98–102, 104, 146; rule of law in, 109–10; trade unions in, 102, 110–11; transition to market economy in, 99–100, 104–5, 112, 136, 146–47; unemployment in, 99, 104, 110–11

Decommunization (lustration), 81, 108–9
Demagogue, potential for rise of, 7
Democracy: capitalism and, 105; in the Czech Republic, 142–43, 146–47; economic prosperity and, 21–22, 48; in Hungary, 142; mass media and, 22; personal values and, 53; in Poland, 91, 142–43, 146; precommunist past and, 72, 75, 119–20; private property and, 4, 22–23, 105; prospects for, 141–47; role of Western countries in transition to, 130; in Russia, 49, 122–23, 143, 145–46; in Slovenia, 142; transition to market economy and, 20–22, 24, 34–36
Diasporas, impact of, 27
Disability pensions, 89–90, 94
Duma (Russia), 49, 51

Eastern Europe, 3, 13, 114–15
East Germany, 14, 39–40, 128
Economic gradualism, 34
Economic power, dispersion of, 22. *See also* Privatization
Economic prosperity, 21–22, 48, 82–83. *See also* Rise in expectations
Economic refugees, 123
Educational systems, role of, 5, 25–26, 129
Egalitarian values in Russia, 58–59
Electoral systems, proportional, 4, 29, 43–44, 79
Émigrés, returning, 26–27
Employee-buyout in Russia, 61
Energy companies, privatization of, 56
Estonia, 142
Ethnic conflict, 85, 108
European Union (EU), 126, 128–32

The Federalist Papers, 37
Federation, advantages of, 10
Finland, 115
Foreign assistance, 121–23, 127–30, 134, 136–37
Foreign debt, 64, 134–36
Foreigners, response to, 27
Foreign investment, 64, 89, 112–13, 121, 124–25, 139

Foreign trade, 64, 91, 112, 124, 130, 135

Freedom Union, 84

Gazprom, 56
Gorbachev, Mikhail, 14, 47
Government of National Understanding, 103
Group of Seven, 133

Havel, Vaclav, 81, 103, 110
Hungary: democracy in, 142; disability and old-age pensions in, 94; economic reforms in, 97; foreign investment in, 89, 113, 125, 135; hyperinflation in, 95; North Atlantic Treaty Organization and, 133–34; privatization in, 86
Hyperinflation, 90, 95

Inflation, 63, 90, 95, 99
International environment, 125–26
International Monetary Fund (IMF), 64, 127–28, 130, 134
International trade, 64, 91, 112, 124, 130, 135
Investment capital, 89. *See also* Foreign investment

Justice and fairness: in the Czech Republic, 81, 109–10; democratic rule and, 8, 38; in East Germany, 81; mercy and, 38, 80; in Poland, 80–82; in Russia, 50, 65; transition and, 37–39

KGB, 57
Kievan Rus, 5
Klaus, Vaclav, 37, 103–7, 110, 112
Kwaśniewski, Aleksander, 79, 82–83

Law, rule of, 31, 53–54, 87, 109–10

Living standards, in East Germany, 39. *See also* Rise in expectations
Lustration (decommunization), 81, 108–9

Mafia in Russia, 55–56
Market economy: desirability of, 19–20; in precommunist past, 2, 4, 75, 119–20; transition to (*see* Transition to market economy)
Market socialism, 18
Marshall Plan, 127, 144–45
Mass media, democracy and, 22
Mazowiecki, Tadeusz, 80–81, 110
Mercy, justice and, 38, 80. *See also* Justice and fairness
Michnik, Adam, 8, 80–81, 110
Middle class, 54, 56, 101–2
Military industry, 59, 122, 130
Military threat from Eastern Europe, 122, 126
Mixed economies, competition in, 24
Morality, 81–82, 109–10

Nationalism, transformation and, 6
Nomenklatura, 18, 59–60, 68, 80–81, 87
North Atlantic Treaty Organization (NATO), 27–28, 132–34
Nuclear threat, 122

Old-age pensioners, in Poland, 85, 89–90, 94
Oleksy, Józef, 80, 109
Organization of Economic Cooperation and Development (OECD), 133

Partial transformation, 17–19
Party of Democratic Socialism (PDS), 40
Pawlak, Waldemar, 87
Peasants' Party, in Poland, 84, 87

Personal values: competition and, 28–29; in the Czech Republic, 105–6, 109–10; democracy and, 53; in Poland, 28–29, 76–77, 146; in Russia, 55, 57–59, 146

PHARE (Poland-Hungary Aid for Restructuring the Economy), 129

Pilsudski, Marshal Jozef, 78

Poland, 71–91; agriculture in, 86, 88; church and state in, 53; constitution of, 72, 74, 77, 83; corruption in, 75–76, 82; decommunization in, 81, 108–9; democracy in, 91, 142–43, 146; electoral system in, 4, 30; foreign debt in, 135–36; investment in, 89, 113, 135, 139; justice and fairness in, 80–82; *nomenklatura* in, 80–81, 87; North Atlantic Treaty Organization and, 133–34; old-age pensioners in, 85, 89–90, 94; personal values in, 28–29, 76–78, 146; political parties in, 77–79, 84, 87; rise in expectations in, 73; role of precommunist past in, 72–75; transition to market economy in, 86–88, 90; unemployment in, 84, 86, 88–90

Poland-Hungary Aid for Restructuring the Economy (PHARE), 129

Police forces, in Russia, 57. *See also* Decommunization

Political mistrust and cynicism, 31

Political parties, 30, 52, 77–79, 84, 87, 102–3

Political stability, 7, 25, 29–32, 65

Polnische Wirtschaft, 73

Poverty, 32, 84

Price liberalization, 35, 60, 112

Private property: in the Czech Republic, 105; democracy and, 4, 22–23; in Russia, 50, 57, 62–63

Privatization: of agriculture, 51, 57 (*see also* Agriculture); in the Czech Republic, 86, 88, 112–13; democracy and, 22–23, 105; in East Germany, 39–40; of energy companies, 56; in Estonia, 86; in Hungary, 86; in Lithuania, 86; in Poland, 80, 84, 86–88, 113; in Russia, 49, 51, 60–62, 86; voucher method of, 112–13

Profit making, 8–9, 55

The Protestant Ethic and the Spirit of Capitalism, 28

Protestantism, 28

Public opinion, in Russia, 50

Refugees, economic, 123

Religious institutions, 5, 26, 53, 76–78

Rise in expectations: after fall of communism, 14, 30; in the Czech Republic, 106–7; in Poland, 73; political stability and, 7, 25, 65

Roman Catholic Church, 5, 26, 76–78

Romania, 134

Russia, 47–65; agriculture in, 49, 51, 62–63, 113; capital flight from, 56, 61, 134; church and state in, 53; corruption in, 54–56, 64, 67; criminal organizations in, 55–56; foreign debt in, 64, 134; justice and fairness in, 50, 65; loss of faith in market economy in, 19; North Atlantic Treaty Organization and, 132–34; personal values in, 55, 57–59, 146; private property in, 49–51, 57, 60–63, 86; robber capitalism in, 143; role of precommunist past in, 16, 50–51, 55; transition to democracy, 49, 122–23, 143, 145–46; transition to market economy, 49, 143, 145; unemployment in, 59, 62–64, 69

Sachs, Jeffrey, 124
Safety-net issues, 32, 84
Schmidt, Helmut, 144–45
Screening (decommunization), 81,
    108–9
Slovakia, 101, 107–8, 146
Slovenia, 134, 142
Smith, Adam, 38
Solidarity, 83–84
Solzhenitsyn, Alexander, 57
Soros, George, 55, 130, 143–44
Soviet Union, 13–14, 95
Standard of living, 19, 23, 49–50. *See
    also* Rise in expectations
State Duma (Russia), 49, 51
State-owned property, finding buyers
    for, 20. *See also* Privatization
Suchocka, Hanna, 4

Tax collection, 63, 82
"Third road" to transformation, 17–19
Third World, private ownership in, 23
Trade unions, 59, 84, 102, 110–11
Transformation of postcommunity so-
    cieties: importance of precommu-
    nist past in, 15–16, 119–20,
    141–42; rate of change needed,
    32–36, 39–40, 104–6, 131; scope
    of change needed, 17–18; sequenc-
    ing of, 34–36
Transition to market economy: in Al-
    bania, 4; authoritarian regimes dur-
    ing, 19–22, 34–35, 37; com-
    prehensive, 20–22, 32; in the
    Czech Republic, 99–100, 104–5,
    112, 136, 146–47; democracy and,
    20–22, 24, 34–36, 83; historical
    prerequisites to, 120; measures of,
    90, 135; partial, 17–20, 24; in Po-

land, 86–88, 90; prospects for,
    141–47; role of Western countries
    in, 121–27; in Russia, 49, 143,
    145; sequencing of, 34–36. *See
    also* Market Economy; Privatiza-
    tion
Treuhandanstalt, 39
Trust, importance of, 54, 66

Ukraine, 123, 134
Unemployment: under communism,
    18; in the Czech Republic, 99,
    104, 110–11; in Poland, 84, 86,
    88–90; in Russia, 59, 62–64, 69
United States Agency for Interna-
    tional Development (USAID), 129

The Velvet Revolution, 103, 136
Vested interests, 8, 37, 131
Visegrad states, 72
Vision for change, 125

Wałesa, Lech, 82
Wealth of Nations, 38
Weber, Max, 28
Western countries: approach to post-
    communist Eastern Europe, 119–
    37; interest in Eastern Europe
    success, 121–24, 136–37; responsi-
    bility toward Eastern Europe, 124,
    144
West Germany, assistance to East
    Germany, 128, 144
World Bank, 64, 127–28, 130, 134
World Trade Organization, 64, 134

Yeltsin, Boris, 47–48, 58, 122
Yugoslavia, 95

About the Author

ROBERT ZUZOWSKI is Senior Lecturer in the Department of International Relations of the University of the Witwatersrand in Johannesburg, South Africa. Among his earlier publications is *Political Dissent and Opposition in Poland* (Praeger, 1992). He has published numerous articles on East European politics in Australia, the United States, Canada, and South Africa.

ISBN 0-275-96145-1

90000>

EAN

9 780275 961459

HARDCOVER BAR CODE